The New Africa Initiative
Working for Synergy

Proceedings of the 1997, Addis Abeba, Ethiopia
and
the 1998, Nairobi, Kenya Workshops

Edited by
Tegegne Teka

OSSREA Development Research Report - No. 2

Organization for
Social Science
Research in
Eastern and
Southern Africa
(OSSREA)

January 2000
Addis Abeba, Ethiopia

OSSREA acknowledges the support of the Ford Foundation Office for Eastern Africa.

Text Layouts: *Misrak Kinfemichael*

Organization for Social Science Research in Eastern and Southern Africa
P. O. Box 31971, Addis Ababa, Ethiopia
Tel.: 00-251-1-551163 Fax: 00-251-1-551399
E-mail: ossrea@telecom.net.et

Printed by Commercial Printing Enterprise, P. O. Box 209, Addis Ababa, Ethiopia

Table of Contents

Preface

The New Africa Initiative (NAI) was initiated in July 1996 in Uganda with the support of the Nairobi-based Ford Foundation's Governance and Civil Society Program for Eastern Africa. The idea was to advance mutually beneficial interaction among key governmental, civil society and knowledge-generating institutions and individuals. The ideas carried over by each institution and the objectives set by the same are indeed very broad.

Six institutions launched various programmes in Entebbe, Uganda, at a workshop held in 1996 to achieve the above objectives. The six institutions were Kituo Cha Katiba: the East African Centre for Constitutional Development (EACODEV); the Series on Alternative Research in East Africa Trust (SAREAT); Development Through Media (DTM); East African Uongozi Institute (EAFUI); the National Museums of Kenya (NMK); and the Organization for Social Science Research in Eastern and Southern Africa (OSSREA).

The Entebbe workshop was preceded by a planning workshop on *"Summer School for Promising Undergraduate Students in East Africa"* convened and hosted by OSSREA in March 1996 in Addis Abeba, Ethiopia. Those who were invited to the planning meeting were senior university administrators, deans of social science and heads of political science departments in Addis Abeba University, Dar es Salaam University, Makerere University and Nairobi University. The planning workshop on the Summer School underlined the need to find alternatives to an African leadership that is self-centered and self-servicing, and that contributes little to develop responsible citizenship.

One observes that the present leadership in Africa has been the management of crisis while the generation of leadership that follows is occupied with the process of indigenization of the system of governance. It is perhaps fair to state that both categories of leadership have failed to consolidate peace, provide the necessary emergency relief in times of difficulty, and put their countries on the path of sustainable development. Not only that but also because of the attempts by the present to assume dominance and high tension have been major characteristic of the political life in the continent. Conspicuous among these are ethnic tensions where ethnicity has been used as a tool for mobilization of support by those who want to stay in power or to acquire new fields of dominance. However, the reality of the situation is that ethnic tensions have led, in some cases, to the collapse of the state and the disintegration of nations.

One major problem that faces Africa in general and East Africa in particular is the lack of leadership that has the vision of taking this part of the continent into the fast changing world. Very few of the leaders seem to know what they would like to achieve concerning the quality of life of their people. They have resisted any attempts for the democratization of the decision-making processes and liberalization of the economy when they are not sure about the favours that their close supporters and/or ethnic group members shall receive. Given the present age of globalization, the problems of the new millennium are going to be very different from those so far encountered by the earlier and the present leadership of East Africa.

The New Africa Initiative is also motivated by the consideration that, despite significant moves towards more open governments in East Africa over the past couple of years, state politics and civil society remain rooted in the authoritarian legacy of colonialism and local traditions of patriarchy. This climate of opinion strongly challenges the next generation of East Africans to have clear thinking and insight to advance the concepts and practices of democratic governance in order to shape the future of the region.

Since the late 1980s, major political, economic, and social changes have been taking place in East Africa. Constitutional transformation that could pave the way to democracy and pluralism has become the order of the day. East Africans are still debating over constitutional choices. Poverty, illiteracy, disease, unemployment continue to bring suffering to the majority of East Africans. As in many countries of Africa, unemployment, hopelessness, disillusionment and frustration have continued to affect the East African youth.

The conflict between the constitutional choices of nationalist leaders and those of civil society groups has manifested itself particularly in the East African countries since the 1990s. This development has put disagreements over constitutional choices at the forefront and brought about that of the governance debate in Africa. The New Africa Initiative programs are meant to contribute to constitution-making and to broaden and strengthen the democratic content of society.

Since the late 1980s, individuals, organisations, institutions and communities in Kenya, Uganda and Tanzania have started to remake societies. New community initiatives, leaders and alternative resources are emerging outside state politics. These initiatives, leaders and resources have a background of gender, racial, national, ethnic and religious diversity. These developments demonstrate not only the making of a new Africa but also the culmination of a political process which has been taking root since the end of the Cold War in particular and the end of colonial rule in general.

Convinced of these developments, the University of Dar es Salaam, Makerere University, University of Nairobi, University of California (James S. Coleman African Studies Centre), Centre for Basic Research, Institute for Policy Analysis and Research (Kenya), East Africa Law Society, East Africa Cooperation Secretariat, Law Society of Kenya and OSSREA, to mention just a few, participated in the Entebbe, Uganda, Workshop in launching the New Africa Initiative.

The New Africa Initiative is meant to help achieve the formation of the 'New African'. An African that would recognize the changes that are taking place in the environment around us. People are now living in a changing world setting. Issues such as globalization, regionalization, HIV-AIDS, etc., are examples that are common to many African countries. As many said in the Workshop, the Initiatives are not issues for East Africa alone but for Africa as a whole. The Initiative is for all Africans or for those who would like to see the recreation of a New Africa by New Africans.

The mandate for facilitating the realization of the objectives of the New Africa Initiative was given to OSSREA. The First Workshop for Synergy on the Initiative was held in Addis Abeba in October 1997 and the Second Workshop was held in October 1998 in Nairobi. OSSREA was assigned a facilitative role, a strategic role of creating synergy among the active players in the formation of the 'New African'.

The New Africa Initiative : Working for Synergy is a project that was dealt with co-operatively by organisations with a view to fostering a creative, tolerant and democratic culture in the younger sections of the population in East Africa, specifically in Kenya, Tanzania and Uganda. It is the idea of promoting democratic constitution and good governance and overall people-based political environment that emerged in the region that inspired the creation of the New Africa Initiative. The publication of this document is therefore intended to make others understand the ideas and the objectives laid down, the issues discussed and the tentative conclusions reached at the two workshops. The 1997 NAI Synergy Workshop in Addis Abeba was organised by the Facilitator, Ms. MaryKay Penn and Venzen Ross Consulting (USA) in collaboration with OSSREA in Addis Abeba and the Ford Foundation in Nairobi. The 1998 NAI Synergy Workshop in Nairobi was organised by the Facilitator, Dr. Tegegne Teka, Regional Project Co-ordinator, OSSREA, Addis Abeba.

Tegegne Teka
Facilitator

Acknowledgements

It is necessary to mention the names and commitments of various individuals and institutions for the successful accomplishment of the New Africa Initiative project. People in-charge of Kituo cha Katiba: East African Centre for Constitutional Development, Series on Alternative Research in East Africa Trust, Development Through Media, East African Uongozi Institute, the National Museums of Kenya, Organisation for Social Science Research in Eastern and Southern Africa, UCLA, and the Nairobi Office of the Ford Foundation deserve special thanks for what they did to promote the objectives of the New Africa Initiative. Ms. Harriet Busingye, Mr. Mutahi Ngunyi, Prof. Rwekaza Mukandala, Ms. Dommie Yambo-Odotte, Dr. Mohamed Isahakia, Dr. Sultan Somjee, Prof. Edmond Keller, Prof. Abdel Ghaffar M. Ahmed, Prof. Jonathan Moyo, Ms. MaryKay Penn, Ms. Assumpta Oturu, Ms. Zainab Ali, Ms. Misrark Kinfemichael and Dr. Tegegne Teka helped in the development and the success of the workshops at various levels. Dr. Kassahun Berhanu and Mr. Shiferaw Bekele, both from the Addis Abeba University, helped in the organisation of the manuscripts into a book. Mrs. Alemtsehay Zewde helped in the development of the book cover design. Ms. Misrark Kinfemichael of OSSREA provided all the necessary secretarial work for this publication. We thank them all for their contributions.

Acronyms

DTM	-	Development Through Media
EACODEV	-	East African Centre for Constitutional Development
EAFUI	-	East African Uongozi Institute
NAI	-	New Africa Initiative
NMK	-	National Museums of Kenya
OSSREA	-	Organization for Social Science Research in Eastern and Southern Africa
SAREAT	-	Series on Alternative Research in East Africa Trust
UCLA	-	University of California – Lost Angeles

1

INTRODUCTIONS AND WORKSHOP OVERVIEW

SESSION ONE: WORKSHOP OFFICIAL OPENING

Chairperson: **Professor Abdel Ghaffar M. Ahmed**
Executive Secretary, OSSREA

Speakers: **Dr. Katherine Pearson,** *Ford Foundation*
Dr. Mohamed Isahakia, *Director General, National Museums of Kenya*
Professor Jonathan Moyo, *University of the Witwatersrand*
Dr. Tade Aina, *Programme Officer, Ford Foundation*
Dr. Tegegne Teka, *Regional Project Coordinator, OSSREA & Facilitator of the New Africa Initiative Workshop*

SUMMARY

The New Africa Initiative: Working for Synergy workshop commenced with welcoming remarks from the Facilitator, Dr. Tegegne Teka, Regional Project Co-ordinator of OSSREA. He outlined the workshop guidelines and the expectation for the two-day gathering. Professor Abdel Ghaffar Ahmed, the Session Chair, made a brief introductory statement and proceeded with the business of the day. He also took a moment and spoke as Secretary General of OSSREA to remind the participants how the New Africa Initiative (NAI) started, the involvement of OSSREA at its early stage, the meeting in Addis Abeba, followed by the meeting in Entebbe. He also mentioned the first workshop that OSSREA hosted in October 1997 in Addis Ababa. In the last two years, he said, OSSREA had nursed NAI and now the time had come for the NAI to stand on its own feet.

Professor Ahmed then asked Dr. Katherine Pearson, the Representative of the Ford Foundation and the funding organization of the NAI, to address the workshop.

In a rather an informal speech, Dr. Pearson welcomed the participants, sharing with them what had happened to her, upon arrival at Safari Park. This seemed to be Dr. Pearson's humorous way of informing the group of what else was going on, on the same grounds, as NAI met. Dr. Pearson mistakenly gone to the *"Constitutional Meeting"* where the Kenyan MPs and the President of Kenya, Daniel Arap Moi was expected.

"How ironic is it!" She said that the President is in the same location. "There is no connection between NAI Workshop to the Constitutional meeting of the MPs. Shouldn't we really be meeting together?" She asked, "shouldn't there be closeness between the two groups as we meet?"

With those few words, Dr. Pearson took the liberty to recognize her colleague from the Ford Foundation; Dr. Jonathan Moyo, who was with the Foundation prior to my coming. "We overlapped for only a month. But I know this is part of his work. He is part of the NAI. It was his work as a program officer." She referred to Dr. Tade Aina who had taken over from Jonathan at the Ford Foundation, as someone who knew everyone in East and West Africa. "He is a gold mine of information about the people and events from the region, and so, I acknowledge both of you and say, how glad I am to have been able to work with you, Jonathan and Tade."

Dr. Pearson acknowledged the presence of the Secretary General of OSSREA, Prof. Ahmed. *"OSSREA, of course, has been birthing and mid-wifing this project,"* she said as she recognized the other key parts of NAI. Dr. Mohamed Isahakia and others in his organization; from *Uongozi* Institute in Dar-es-Salaam, Professor Mukandala and from UCLA, Professor Edmond Keller; Kituo Cha Katiba or the Constitutional Centre for Eastern Africa, DTM and SAREAT.

As she will not be able to participate in the two-day meeting, she informed the group that Tade and Jonathan were there to cover for her. *"You all have a wonderful time the next couple of days,"* she said and *" I know you are doing a very important work, and it is a pleasure to be here and thank you for having me."*

Professor Ahmed thanked Dr. Pearson, and then called on Dr. Mohammed Isahakia, Director General of National Museums of Kenya (NMK), also Chair of the Steering Committee of the NAI to speak on the Committee's activities for 1997-98.

Good Morning, Ladies and Gentlemen,

"For those of you who were in the last workshop in Addis. You'll recall that one of the major recommendations that came out of the meeting towards the end was; the need to establish some sort of a "Steering Committee" that would coordinate the activities of the various programs, rather in an informal manner. With the main objective of promoting synergy, which at that workshop, and even in today's workshop, continues to be the major theme.

"I was appointed as the first chairperson of this "Steering Committee", whose membership is essentially made up of the various key program coordinators that constitute the NAI. The Steering Committee as I said, has its main aim; to promote synergy, partnership, networking both within the program elements, but also with outside institutions and bodies which have the same aims and objectives.

"The membership of the Committee include Dr. Mukandala , *Dr. Keller of UCLA, who most of you know, have significant role in NAI. It also has Jonathan Moyo, who previously was Program Officer at the Ford Foundation and now project manager at the University of Witwatersrand and OSSREA represented by Dr. Teka.*

"What I would like to emphasize is the nature of this Steering Committee? It is simply a very loose arrangement that was set in place with the consent of the members whose main aim is to help in facilitating the coordination of the various elements of NAI. We have not been very visible over much of the year because there wasn't much progress made in many of the programs. Hopefully, in the course of the next year, we will begin to see much more closer networking, exchange of information, and the general enhancement of awareness among all of us with the aim of sustaining this program.

"Last evening, we had a meeting, and I would like to take the pleasure to introduce the new chairperson, Dr. Mukandala, Chairman of Uongozi School in Dar-es-Salaam who will now be responsible for coordinating the activities of the Steering Committee. With those few remarks, what I would like to do is to welcome all of you to this workshop. It is certainly going to be a very exciting workshop over the next two days. There is a lot of progress that each one of us will be reporting. On Wednesday, we have made arrangements for those of you, who have not been to our Museum here, to visit our Museum, and see some of the work that we've put into place, particularly, the exhibit on conflict resolution and peace making. Thank you very much".

After thanking Dr. Isahakia, for the information he had given the group on the Steering Committee, Professor Ahmed made a few remarks before introducing, Professor. Jonathan Moyo.

Our next speaker, Professor Ahmed said, is a person who conceived the idea of the NAI. An observation he said, he had made having read the documents, and having had correspondence with Professor Moyo. *"The NAI had been a sort of a promotion of an idea, Professor Moyo had started way back at the University of Zimbabwe, before coming to the Ford Foundation. 'I hope I am right,' Prof. Ahmed noted, I think that is the assumption I have made from reading some of the introductions. He developed this further to this kind of program, and he has nursed it very carefully. I think with a lot of effort, running around, corresponding with people, trying to put them together, to cope with wild ideas that spring in these meetings and put them in streamline."* Professor Jonathan Moyo, who was with the Ford Foundation is now with University of Witwatersrand in South Africa and he is still with you as a partner of the NAI.

Professor Moyo - *"Observations on the Making of a New Africa: Opportunities and Challenges for East Africa"*

Professor Moyo thanked the organizers for having invited him. He was happy to be at the workshop as a free person, and not as program officer. And following Prof. Ahmed's remarks that he (Prof. Moyo) had conceived the idea of the Initiative, Prof. Moyo told the group that it was time to set the record right.

"The NAI was not started by the Ford Foundation," he said, *"because the Foundation is not in the business of starting things like this. But rather,"* he noted, *"in the business of identifying what initiatives are out there, and seeking out people who are marginalized."* It was the environment in East Africa that made the NAI possible. The climate of debate and the issues people were discussing then, facilitated the emergence of the components that now constitute the NAI. The issues that had brought about such a debate were; in Tanzania for example, 'the Bill of Rights', in Uganda, 'No Party State', and in Kenya, the question of 'the New Constitution'.

Prof. Moyo then proceeded to outline how each component of the Initiative had responded to the different aspects of the debate and changes in East Africa.

UONGOZI SCHOOL

The new challenge facing the universities in East Africa then called for a common forum. A forum that would re-capture the cooperation that had existed between the East African Universities. According to Prof. Moyo, events of the recent past had interrupted that process, the 'one-party state', university closures (Nairobi and Dar-es-Salaam), and the disruption of Makerere. *Uongozi* School becomes a basis for the revival of such dialogue, and also a platform, upon where future leaders can speak a common language about issues of common concern to the region. The University of California, Los Angeles, UCLA inclusion in this component was important, because it gave recognition to the earlier connection between UCLA and East African Universities. Many of the African Scholars noted Prof. Moyo had some association with UCLA. Also, the current global environment he said made this connection necessary.

SERIES ON ALTERNATIVE RESEARCH IN EAST AFRICA TRSUT (SAREAT)

SAREAT on the other hand, was born from the desire of young generations of East African scholars, who wanted to emulate what was going on in other regions of the continent. In Southern Africa for instance, there were research institutions focusing on issues of concern to the region, SAPES based in Harare, Zimbabwe and in West Africa, CODESRIA were cases in point.

THE NATIONAL MUSEUMS OF KENYA (NMK)

The NMK was unique, because Museums are known for preserving the past culture. And people like Dr. Somjee are said to be the preservers of the past. The NMK de-mystifies that because of the need today to re-visit the issues, which will help our understanding of the present, and resolve some the question of ethnic differences. This new role of the Museum was recognized when Dr. Somjee caught the attention at the African Studies Association in Ohio during a forum organized by UCLA.

DEVELOPMENT THROUGH MEDIA (DTM)

FORGOTTEN LOT, the film project of DTM, addresses an important aspect in the South Africa struggle---the participation of generations; those who took part in the struggle, and those left behind, but are struggling in a different form. The project also articulates the contribution of East Africa, which the world knows nothing about. Nyerere made the South Africans at home, and they become part of Tanzanian civil society. So, this media is a forum that talks about that story and what that contribution was about.

FORGOTTEN LOT, was also relevant to the current debate in South Africa. The question of citizenship, as you know, South African constitution is the most liberal constitution in the world. So, the transition in South Africa is much more pronounced than the rest of Africa. Also, as South Africa undergoes leadership transition, Vice-president, Mbeki talks about New Africa----African Renaissance. It is about "Africa Rising". Prof. Moyo summarized the issues in the following eight points:

1. The timing of South African re-birth, at the end of the century. This is seen as the beginning time for mankind. It is the re-examination of where we have been and where we are going.
2. There is a need for a debate about the presumed end of colonial Africa, and time has come for the first time to re-define and construct a new identity.
3. With the birth of a new South Africa, it is presumed that racism has ended in Africa. Now, the debate about new identity, the new African.
4. As South Africa goes through a leadership transition, there is also a talk of a new breed of leaders; Mbeki, Museveni and Rawlings.
5. The whole idea of democratic movement and multiparty.
6. The belief that African states will no longer be driven by politics, but by a new liberal economic that is market driven.
7. The question of globalization, as it re-defines Africa, are these new opportunities or are these problems for the continent?
8. The rise of a new social movement.

As a result of the debate in South Africa, Prof. Moyo noted some other issues that had come about; the whole question about who is an African? What is the place of Africa in the world? How can Africa change the world or the world change Africa?

Professor Ahmed found Prof. Moyo's speech as having presented some issues, which could be incorporated into a new agenda. But critical analysis had to be given to what would constitute that agenda, so it can be of significance to the Initiative. Professor Ahmed then introduced Dr. Tade Aina, Program Officer, Ford Foundation, whom he said had previously worked with CODESRIA, and had lot to offer to the region. *"We are happy to have him around and we'll benefit from him."*

DR. TADE AINA, *"NAI : A VISION FOR SUSTAINABILITY"*

I am taking a baton from Prof. Moyo, and now have to move forward. I am happy with the remarks by Prof. Moyo that the Initiative came from the people. It was not the *"Livingstone"* discovery. The Ford Foundation only facilitated and coordinated the making of the Initiative. The Initiative Dr. Aina said was a partnership, and he urged the partners to work together, and take what everyone was doing with commitment, conviction and belief. Africans must believe and have conviction that a new Africa is emerging from our experience.

Prof. Ahmed thanked Dr. Aina for his brief comment and expressed the hope that Dr. Aina would continue to help the Initiative. Dr. Teka followed with a speech on the role of OSSREA.

DR. TEKA - *"OSSREA's ROLE IN THE NAI & WORKSHOP GOALS"*

Dr. Teka thanked the chair, and said OSSREA was more a facilitator for the co-partners. OSSREA was there to encourage partners to do more, and to come together because everything depended on their achievements. OSSREA, he said was interested in expanding the awareness of the Initiative to other African countries, and so other partners in other parts of Africa had been invited to the workshop. It was important he noted because *"these projects* are *our projects, our children's projects, and every African's projects."*

He then elaborated further on the role OSSREA had played in the past two years. OSSREA, Dr. Teka said had lived up to its responsibilities, OSSREA organized the last two workshops; last year in Addis and today in Nairobi. Therefore, it was last year that the Initiative partners would come together under OSSREA's facilitation.

Dr. Teka then proceeded to announce some program changes and invited all participants to sign-up for the visit to the NMK.

Prof. Ahmed thanked Dr. Teka for facilitating the meeting activities for the past two years. The *"infant is now walking"*, he said. OSSREA was happy to have provided support. And seeing that the workshop had commenced on a very enlightening note, Prof. Ahmed wished the participants good luck in their deliberations.

COMMENTS AND OBSERVATIONS/POSSIBLE AREAS FOR SYNERGY

1. The comments by Dr. Pearson about the *"Constitutional Conference"* of the MPs taking place on the same grounds with the NAI, but having no connection, raises crucial issues for the Initiative partners. Mainly, the need for relevance, and develop linkages within the East African environment. It means NAI had to move beyond the confines of research and workshops into the arena of visibility in relation to issues being debated in the region.

2. However, the comments can also be read to be more specific in relation to *KITUO CHA KATIBA,* whose function probably needs to be expanded to include mechanisms and structures for monitoring activities in each country, as such activities related to constitutional-making or constitutionalism. In so doing, *KITUO CHA KATIBA,* would be part or the organizer, and so basically, *KITUO CHA KATIBA*, would avoid being an outsider, or being overtaken by events. It means *KITUO CHA KATIBA,* needs to have linkages with those very institutions that *KITUO CHA KATIBA,* seeks to transform. The challenge then for *KITUO CHA KATIBA,* is for it to become East Africa's eye-lenses into the future and could set the agenda issues.

3. To achieve 1) and 2) *KITUO CHA KATIBA,* needs have joint collaboration other components for the NAI, particularly SAREAT, which was doing a lot on constitution-making and constitutionalism.

4. From the report of the Chairman of the Steering Committee, the Committee needs to be strengthened. The current loose arrangement limits the Committee's function and responsibilities. As such, the Committee would be in a better position to define the agenda for the annual of meetings of the partners beyond just issues of synergy; but on how to move forward, how to become more relevant to the changing conditions in the region. So, the annual meeting becomes a forum not just for reporting on past activities, but also be the platform, where concrete issues on the future challenge for the Initiative partners are defined.

5. The Steering Committee should also be a body that energizes the Initiative partners, strengthening their work, identifies and assists in providing solutions to program weak areas.

6. On the present debate in South Africa the eight points challenged NAI partners to find relevance. How do these issues enhance the thinking within the Initiative? How does the NAI also influence the South African debate? How does the new East Africa relate to the evolving Africa in general, and does this broad thinking for a new definition of Africa also try to place the continent in her rightful place in the global arena.

SESSION TWO: PRESENTATION BY UONGOZI INSTITUTE.

Chairperson: **Prof. Njuguna Ngethe,** *Institute of Policy Analysis and Research, UoN*
Rapporteur: **Ms. Bernadetta Killan,** *EAFUI*
Presenter: **Prof. Rwekaza Mukandala,** *Uongozi School*

Prof. Mukandala started by addressing the question; why Uongozi Institute is important? The institute is important in order to solve the problem that is characterized by the absence of dynamism initiative and vision among leaders.

He stated five objectives of the East African Uongozi Institute

1. Giving over 200 selected students leadership skills
2. Increasing knowledge on leadership-related problems
3. Creating network of information dissemination
4. Providing advisory and mid-career follow-up training to EAFUI graduates and other interested public servants in the region.
1. Developing a global critical constituency support.

Prof. Mukandala further stated that EAFUI's mission will be implemented through the following strategies, namely,

1. The Uongozi school
2. Networking with different stakeholders
3. UCLA coordinated activities.

He explained specific activities of the 1998 Uongozi School that included educational visits made, recruitment of students in respective universities and qualifications of applicants. The composition of students was as follows: 24 – (57%) Females and 18 – (43%) Males.

There were 4 universities that formed Uongozi School of 1998, namely; University of Dar es Salaam, University of Nairobi, Makerere University, American Universities and University of Copenhagen.

Apart from educational visits the programme included formal studies covering wide range of issues under the main theme of Governance, Democracy and Development. There were 32 resource persons of which 8 were females and 24 were males.

The Institute's future directions fall under four main strategies, namely,

1) The Uongozi school
2) Research, Publications and Documentation
3) Networking and Information Dissemination
4) Advisory and Follow-up Training Services.

Prof. Mukandala also stated how the objectives of the Institute will be measured and assessed.

In terms of sustaining the Institute in the long run, Prof. Mukandala mentioned various ways including:

1) Mobilization of financial support from donors mainly the Ford Foundation that is currently supporting the objectives of EAFUI.
2) Mobilization for funding from national government budgets through the auspices of cooperating universities.
3) Mobilization of support from private and voluntary organizations in East Africa.
4) Collection of fees from foreign and some local students that will be able pay.
5) Sale of EAFUI publications
6) Fees from advisory services and training of mid-career leaders and public servants.

He finally supports the idea of establishing synergy and the institute intends to do the following,

- Inviting partners to participate in the activities of the Institute especially the Uongozi School
- Using research findings and publications of other partners
- Get services from partners e.g.` SAREAT
- Send some students as interns to other partners' projects.

DISCUSSION

1. Prof. Joshua Olewe Nyunya informed the participants of the important role played by the vice-chancellors of the cooperating universities. They were all very supportive of the Institute's mission. Also, the Chief Executive of East African Secretariat was very much keen to be of any assistance to the Institute. He further said that the Uongozi School provided a great opportunity for students interaction and learning. Uongozi School is an important inter- university linkage at student level.

2. Prof. Pearl Robinson gave the following suggestions:

    - The actual curriculum should give more room for student's interactions.
    - Also the school may bring young leaders in their careers to come and talk to students on issues related to difficulties in leadership role.
    - Students should make use of information technology e.g. Internet exploration.
    - The curriculum should include films, novels and plays.

3. The chairperson, Prof. Njuguna Negthe raised the following questions

    - How different was the actual classroom dynamics from a typical university system?
    - Does the Institute have any plans to include students outside universities?

4. Mr. Paulos Chane asked why is it that other African countries are not included in the Institute?

5. A consultant from Rockefeller Foundation/Ford Foundation suggested that students should learn information – retrieval skills from different source e.g. libraries, Internet etc. She is happy to work with the project on this matter.

6. There was a suggestion that the school should include students from other segments of society i.e. civic organizations.

7. Mr. Sabiti Makara asked, How can Uongozi graduates influence others?

8. Dr. John Barya expressed his reservations that there is a conceptual problem with Uongozi school – i.e. is it a training center or a forum for discussing issues? He also asked,

   - What were the mechanisms for testing the objectives of Uongozi School especially that of creating future leaders?

9. Some suggestions were made that given the fact that next years' theme for the school is on 'conflict resolution', arrangements should be made for students to visit refugees camps.

10. Prof. Mujaju cautions of the financial implications of all the suggestions made by the participants.

11. Mr. Nathan Byamukama stated that Human Rights Commission of Uganda is willing to share its publications with the Uongozi School. He also asked about the possibilities of creating a permanent structure for the Uongozi School.

12. Prof. A. G. M. Ahmed asked that why a 25% of USA students in Uongozi school? He also informed the participants of the available OSSREA scholarship for senior scholars who can contribute to the Uongozi programme.

13. Dr. Tade Akin Aina suggested that the Institute should look for linkages with other centers that are doing the same thing e.g. international leadership centers. The institute needs support to achieve its dreams.

14. Prof. Olewe finally stated that all recommendations will be taken seriously by the Institute's Committee.

15. Prof. Mukandala finally responded to some of the issues raised.

    1) The question of information technology is very important in order to facilitate this type of learning. The school has to be located at the University for technology accessibility.

    2) Linking with local communities is important.

3) On expanding recruitment base he said this is extremely difficult as the demand is overwhelming and therefore the choice has to be made.

4) Emphasized the need for having foreign students in the school.

SESSION THREE: PRESENTATION BY THE NATIONAL MUSEUMS OF KENYA

Chairperson: **Dr. John Jean Barya**, *Makerere University, Uganda*
Rapporteur: **Mr. Nathan Byamukama**, *Uganda Human Rights, Uganda*
Presenter: **Dr. Sultan Somjee**, *National Museums of Kenya, Nairobi, Kenya*

Dr. Somjee explained that the National Museums of Kenya have been working on three areas namely: Ethnicity, Religion and Race. He indicated that they have gone to the field, got data and documented them for communication to the public.

It was also reported that the National Museums of Kenya have both worked with pastoralist and agriculturalist communities in Kenya with an objective of pushing for the culture of peace. It was further reported that the current research, the NMK, was engaged in Traditional Modes on Conflict Resolution. Dr. Somjee suggested that there was a need to shift from for example looking at the Masai as Warriors to looking at the Masai methods of conflict resolution. Turning to Religion, Dr. Somjee identified Christianity and Islam as major religions in Kenya. It was pointed out even in Moslem societies, the practices of peace making is different. They approach conflict and peace from their respective cultural background.

Other minorities and their respective cultures were also pointed out as having their own ways of resolving conflicts. An example of Asian-Africa was given as one of the non-indigenous cultures. The pastoralists like the Turkan, Masai, Kenyan Somali and the Pokat were studied to see symbols and rituals that are applied in peace making and how peace is understood and negotiated.

Dr. Somjee observed that in his research he found out that there are peace sites which are recognized locally within local communities but are not recognized nationally. A book published recently which looks at eight different groups and how they resolve conflicts was cited.

The issue of recent bombing in Nairobi and its impact on the Muslim community including the de-registration of some of the Muslim NGOs was highlighted.

It was also pointed out that a large number of Kenyans were illiterate. He observed that visuals were important because visual knowledge is accessible to the illiterates. To this end local artists from Nairobi are being contacted to help in the distribution of visual knowledge and a wider public has so far registered.

It was also reported that the NMK have received encouraging remarks from visitors in the visitors book while also several MA students are doing their theses on indigenous peace keeping traditions.

Regarding publications, it was reported that five articles and a book have been published on the NMK's work. People specially NGOs have used these materials. The NMK also has educational programs for school children where they come and learn from each other's different ethnic groups methods of resolving conflicts.

Artifacts in the museums were cited as instrumental as objects used in conflict resolution.

Women were also cited as respected by all traditions among the warrior communities. An example of a Greenbelt by women which can resolve a conflict was given to stop a fight.

DISCUSSION

- There was a question as to whether there was a way to transmit the information electronically.
- There was also a question as to how the research would get to state officials and also how it will help the whole of East Africa.

At this point Dr. Mohamed Isahakia, also of NMK, explained that they were specifically concerned with knowing how justice is dispensed in these local communities and then in future issues of local understanding of human rights would be studied.

- Regarding content with state officials, Dr. Isahakia said they work with the local administration. He also noted that there must be need to explore and harmonize transnational traditions between Kelangong and the Turkana in Uganda and Kenya respectively and also the Oromos in

Kenya and Ethiopia. He said that he saw an opportunity in working with Uongozi School.

There was also an issue of arms trafficking in these pastoral communities like the Kelangong and the Turkanas and the conflicts between them. The question was what type of conflict will each address inter or intra conflict?

- A question was also asked about the relationship between traditional and government/state forms.

- A comment was also made to the effect that much as we are putting conditional forms of conflict resolution to the museums it seems the African cultures too were going to the museums after being disseminated by western culture. Safeguards for our cultures were called.

Dr. Somjee replied briefly, first by thanking participants for their comments and questions. He reminded participants that their work was not crisis solving but building on notions of conflicts and peace. The research is concerned with how the conflict is resolved. Participants were told that pastoral groups were engaged in peace synergy and that respective pastoral groups had a hierarchy of the authority ranging from a super being to elder and the blood relation.

SESSION FOUR: PRESENTATION BY THE SERIES ON ALTERNATIVE RESEARCH IN EAST AFRICA TRUST (SAREAT)

Chairperson: **Professor A. B. Mujaju,** *Makerere University*
Rapporteur: **Ms. Assumpta Oturu,** *Radio Station KPFK, USA*
Presenter: **Mr. Mutahi Ngunyi,** *SAREAT*

The Session was a report on the activities of SAREAT since the last meeting in Addis Ababa, Ethiopia in October 1999. Mr. Ngunyi gave a progress report, future directions for SAREAT, its vision and sustainability, including strategies for synergy. A discussion and comments from the participants followed and Mr. Ngunyi responded to most of these inquiries. Some of the participants congratulated Mr. Ngunyi on his excellent production of the magazine, which was distributed to all members.

Mr. Ngunyi began his talk by underscoring the East African crisis. He defined the current changes in two components, one being the *'Multiple Transitions'*, which he articulated in three points:

a) The generation crisis had given rise to issues of succession and revolt of the elders.

b) This revolt had created governments in waiting, and this had brought about the emergence of a new breed of leaders.

c) These new breed of leaders had militarism in their politics, and this had become a way to socialize elders out of power.

The Second component of the crisis Mr. Ngunyi noted was the component of transition.

The constitution-making was at two levels; it was taking place at the national level, where the process of constitution-making was on-going. The different identities, nationalities had come together to make a covenant. In the case of Ethiopia, *"they put together a covenant that was interesting, that allowed different nationalities to form their own countries, if they wanted to."* Now, he said, this was also happening at municipalities, where different nationalities and groups were putting together a process of covenant making. We have seen this in case of Kenya in particular, where groups are coming together to put up rules that are to govern their interaction in regards to water.

The crisis raises from what he referred to as---- *'our connectivity'* as a result of the relationships between a nationalism, ethnicity and identity. The connectivity, he noted was not only on the national level. His observations of this process had come from the on going work among the NGOs in civil society. *"What we've found out from the work we've been doing,"* he said, *"was that there were some kind linkages between the advancement for rights and poverty eradication."* Most people involved in the whole process of social commissioning in development work, were realizing that there were certain issues, given the circumstances which required the understanding of certain rights. Mr. Ngunyi gave the example of women in the slums of Nairobi, who were given access to water. Although the land where the water was located belonged to the government, the politicians grabbed the land. In this case, he said those development agencies involved with the women now found themselves talking about the issues of land rights.

After introducing the issues, Mr. Ngunyi then proceeded to address the challenge facing SAREAT. He summarized SAREAT's activities from December, 1997 as follows:

1) To set out to capture the politics of a given moment in a transition.
2) To seek certain aspects of this particular transitions, and the new way of doing things, and to broadcasting them.
3) To incorporate these aspects (as mentioned in 2) in the process of planning for transition.
4) To state an East African position.

All these had been achieved as listed:

1. We have done a magazine called the *East African Alternatives* (copies were distributed to members). - This has been put together by journalists in the region, and basically talks about political economy, and the transition.
2. We have sample title for book series on Kenya (titles listed in the back of the magazine).
3. We have made a series of working papers that we have produced. (samples were shown)
4. We have put together a web-site in which we display all the materials, magazine and books.

Aside from this, Research Programs to support SAREAT's publications were stipulated as follows:

1. We have had on going programs with the University of Leeds Center for Democratization, and we are calling it the democratic policy.
2. Now we have done a survey of 70 democracy/governance, and human rights organizations in Kenya, and we hope to have the same done in Uganda and Tanzania. The results of the later research will be the publication of a paper on the *'state and civil society in East Africa'*.
3. We have put together proposals for some work, and among them one on civil society building.

On issues of collaborative, Mr. Ngunyi stated the following as a summary of activities for 1997-98.

1. In terms of coalition building, we have done some work with MWENGO, a networking groups for NGOs based in Harare - co-publishing a book.

2. We also have a sabbatical program, for people who are in transition from academia to civil societies or from one civil organization to another. A person can at least take a month or two to go to some kind of reflection and come out with some kind of publications.
3. In April 1998, we had a workshop in Arusha that involved eight countries on constitution-making for Eastern Africa.
4. Tamarin School – a forum where people in Academia, the donor community and NGOs can come together and discuss ideas on poverty, development of civil society in East Africa. We have had discussions in July on civil society in East Africa.

On synergy Mr. Ngunyi spelt out the prospective areas in four points:

1. Internship/SAREAT and the University of Helsinki
2. Hosting the work of the Initiative and linking-up websites
3. Production of newsletter on the initiative activities
4. Solicitation of manuscripts

Dr. Mujaji thanked Mr. Ngunyi for presenting a very wide range of activities, and opened the floor for discussions.

DISCUSSION

Dr John Barya commented by saying that he thinks this is one of the most concrete project in this Initiative. It can even be touched. This is not to say others are not concrete, but this is the most concrete. I don't know, it seems 1) that you are coming out with so many publications at the same time. I don't know if this visible. The monthly review, then the journal, and of course the general publications. I don't know, but is it possible, then that is very good.

The problem of management, the issue of credibility, because once you say you'll come out, you have to be constant. On the program for publishing books, Dr. Barya said it would be useful to coordinate the activities, so that people can relate. At least the Center for Basic Research in Uganda would be interested.

Mr. Geoffrey Tukahebwa thanked Mr. Ngunyi for his presentation and proper insight into the work. He then asked a question relating to politics and economic, *"you to talk about new breed of African leaders, who have taken over power. Are we looking at these African leaders in economic terms, since they have liberalized the economies, and centralized politics?"*

Mr Tukabebwa then reminded Mr. Ngunyi of the dummies he had shown in Addis Ababa whatever happened to them? Because after that, he said we never got the copies of the publication, and then requested Mr. Ngunyi to elaborate further on the question of multiple transition.

Mr. John Aluko Orodho volunteered to assist with the circulation of the journal at the university level.

Dr. Eva Rathegeber (the IDRC) pointed out to Mr. Ngunyi the need to include the journal in the research index for wider research access.

Prof. Moyo suggested to Mr. Ngunyi to consult with Tade because of Dr. Aina's experience in publication. Such consultation could assist Mr. Ngunyi to address the credibility issue. Generally, Prof. Moyo was impressed with the publication and the quality of the material was very important. But he told Mr. Ngunyi that it might be necessary to drop some of the journals.

Dr. Robinson expressed interest in the proverbs, and the possibility of making them available, so she can use them in some of her classes.

Responding to the comments and inquiries, Mr. Ngunyi referred to himself as a toddler running around very aggressively. He said sustainability could not be on SAREAT alone, but also on others doing solid research in various institutions. There is a need to know, who is doing what, and develop communication with SAREAT on their activities. SAREAT he said doesn't have a pool of researchers but can provide the facilities to be able to publish the work. There was a need for participants to support SERAT and work together.

Following Mr. Ngunyi's response, Dr. Tade also congratulated him (Mr. Ngunyi) on the job well done, and cautioned him to be focused. On the question of management capacity, he asked Mr. Ngunyi to consider the following; cost, recovery, circulation, profit/non-profit making. He asked about what was meant by the alternative research, just out of curiosity.

Dr. Keller gave Mr. Ngunyi some advice based on his own earlier accounts on publication agenda. It is hard work, he said, it was important to do market analysis about the competition out there. Dr. Keller then gave examples of journals he had been involved with, namely; *Trans Africa Forum*. The other issue Dr. Keller raised was the need to define an aspect of focus and determine whether this would be an advocacy journal or not. It is therefore very important to identify the niche, he said.

Prof. Mujaju, the Chairperson, also congratulated Mr. Ngunyi on the beautiful work, but asked him to do some occasional paper on Uganda and Tanzania also, and not Kenya alone.

In conclusion, Mr. Ngunyi thanked the participant for their contributions. He said he would continue to consult with Dr. Aina on publications, and pointed out this had already been on going. Mr. Ngunyi said he will take up the issue of indexing, and on Bayra's concerns, he pointed out that he was not working alone, but had commissioned other people to help him with the magazine. On the dummies, he said the issues had been sensitive, but this had been resolved. On the alternate research, he said the journal was seen as an alternate to the research done by outsiders on the region. The research was therefore an alternative to the globalized position.

COMMENTS AND OBSERVATIONS AND POSSIBLE AREAS FOR SYNERGY

1. SAREAT should be a forum for the publication of the work of the Initiative partners, and could also be part of joint research.

2. From the summary of SAREAT activities for the year, constitution-making was one of the areas, if this focus continues, then there should be joint work between *KITUO CHA KATIBA* and SAREAT.

3. The outcome of the research project and the issues of debate in the journal, if reflective of the climate of the day, should be integrated into the yearly syllabus for *Uongozi* School.

SESSION FIVE: PRESENTATION BY THE UNIVERSITY OF CALIFORNIA LOS ANGELES (UCLA) – AFRICAN STUDIES CENTER

Chairperson: **Professor A. B. Mujaju**, *Makerere University*
Rapporteur: **Ms. Assumpta Oturu,** *USA*
Presenter: **Prof. Edmond Keller,** *UCLA, African Studies Center*

SUMMARY

The session focused on the James Coleman African Studies Centre, University of California, Los Angeles. As part of the Initiative, UCLA seemed to play a strategic role that placed NAI into the center of this whole idea of constituency building for Africa in the United States. Professor Edmond Keller's approach to public forums, both at the African Studies Association Conference, and at UCLA, including involvement in the national summits on Africa appeared to be efforts to significantly integrate some aspects of the Initiative. Also, creates awareness for the Initiative with the United States. In a sense, UCLA under the leadership of Professor Edmond Keller opened the door for both East Africans and Americans and for the Initiative, it is a window into the world of the United States of America.

Professor Edmond Keller, "UCLA/African Studies Center"

The New African Initiative was seen in the context of the emerging publications, and efforts of African scholars, who have demonstrated commitment in articulating the African voice. A voice that is engaging the process of globalization----just to name a few examples: the works of Thandika Mkandawire, when he was with CODESRIA and Jonathan Moyo's multi-media project----"*The making of New Africa*". Africans want to engage the process of globalization rather than ignoring it or running away from it and that is what the New Africa Initiative is all about. That coincides with the Ford Foundation's efforts in the past two years.

In the United States, the Ford Foundation has been funding university projects that deal with across borders and build bridges in interdisciplinary sense as well as across cultures. And that seems to be how UCLA to have come to this particular picture. We were already doing some collaborative work with the University of Dar-es-Salaam, the University of Nairobi that how it all began.

UCLA has a couple of grants from the Ford Foundation, one of them is to work with this Synergy Workshop to help develop and disseminate information about the NAI in the United States. In this area, we have worked with Dr. Teka on first Synergy workshop. We also hosted a round table where a number of participants were represented at the last African Studies Association Conference. We had presentations from Dr. Mukandala, Dr. Somjee, myself, Assumpta Oturu, represented DTM and this was to informed American audience about what was going on with the NAI. But not all of NAI was represented, we that changes this year because we are having a round table again. Afterwards, we had a well attended reception.

However, UCLA became involved way earlier on with the synergy workshop on Uongozi Institute. We were called by the program officer at Ford Foundation to sort think about situating UCLA as part of the NAI. So, we

worked very hard, initial with a small grant that Dr. Mukandala managed, we planned, met in Entebbe, and had follow-up meetings in Arusha.
In the early stages of Uongozi School, UCLA provided education materials, and other kinds of educational resources, computer hardware and software, books and we produced the recruitment materials. We recruited students. Again, we had this idea in the United States, and we still do that we need to internationalize our curriculum, and get our students to have first hand experience in living abroad, living in Africa, interacting with Africans. Within such interactions, misconceptions, stereotypes can be overcome. Uongozi Institute serves that purpose of breaking down those barriers, and in essence is the beginning of the building of cooperation and that is what we need to achieve. So, we recruited students from American universities, it was not restricted to any particular nationality, or any particular ethnic group, they just had to be in an American universities.

We also agreed to identify placement opportunities for Uongozi fellows once they had completed their year. We are in the process of doing that now. We have as part of the budget, the ability to fund a few students who participated last year and in East Africa there is a budget also. We have identified places where some of these students might be placed in the United States or in Africa. We simply need to know who the students are and who are to be placed, that is one part that UCLA is doing.

A major aspect that we are doing in the United States is sort of driving into this whole idea of building the constituency for Africa. In the U.S. right now that is a major project. We have a multi-year national summit on Africa, which is broken down into regional summits, they have been two held so far. There are six more to be done over the next few years---all at the local and regional level, UCLA has been a part. We are funded by Ford to organize public education forums, and in those forum what we want to do is to get the African voice on African issues in the American context. Let the Africans speak for themselves and interrogate U.S. policy towards Africa and create a dialogue between Africans and Americans and among Americans themselves. The whole idea is to build a constituency for Africa.

U.S. policy towards Africa has three components:

1) Democracy and human rights
2) Trade and investment
3) Peace and security

And you will not get trade and investment unless you get the other two. Bearing that in mind our public forums concentrate on these three areas of this policy. Our first event is going to be a conference called "Which Way

Nigeria?" It is going to involve Nigerians, who will represent the government position and Nigerians, who represent opposition, various aspects of opposition plus we are going to have representation from the U.S. government and NGOs.

The idea is to get American citizens who are not used to looking at Africa in this way, so they become informed, and if they are informed then they become influential about what is a good U.S. policy towards Africa.

UCLA's involvement with three African universities and all of you in the NAI is a mile in international collaboration. This is what Ford wanted to accomplish, we think, when they articulated this position a couple of years ago. We have proved that we can do this.

Thank you.

DISCUSSION SUMMARY

The question of how to respond the call for globalization, but engaging globalization in the context of local knowledge, and how the process of student interaction at Uongozi Institute provided American Students with a meaningful approach of interrogating American policy towards Africa. It was important for Africa to be seen, and Africa to see itself in the global context noted Professor Keller. In American classrooms, he said students were interrogating U.S policy towards Africa and this can also be done at Uongozi Institute.

The Chairman, Professor Mujaju injected the importance of the theme---building constituency for Africa in the U.S. African-Americans had to work with Congress on African issues. They can do so, just as the Jews have done for Israel. Professor Mujaju said the time had come for increased alliances. He thanked Dr. Keller for his efforts in constituency building for Africa.

Professor Robinson introduced the fact that American peoples' thinking of Africa was beginning to change since President Clinton's visit to Africa earlier in the year. The bombing in East Africa saw American concern about the loss of African lives, but in the media this incident brought back the old coverage of crisis. So, UCLA's coordinating efforts, Professor Robinson said, needed to be increased to effect the necessary change. She noted that Africa's image was currently under siege as talk about wars and things falling apart continued, and because of that a lot of work has to be done. In all this, Dr. Keller saw an opportunity for more dialogue and collaboration.

OBSERVATIONS, COMMENTS, SUGGESTIONS AND SYNERGY ISSUES

1. Aside from what UCLA was already doing in terms of public forum for the Initiative at the African Studies Associations, UCLA could also possibly support the awareness of the published work of the different components of the NAI among the public, and the academic communities within the United States. UCLA could use the already available channels and events could be organized on the different themes. Authors of such works, or researchers, or representatives could be sponsored for speaking engagements.

2. In engaging in constituency building for Africa, UCLA should also extend this to the U.S. media, and begin to organize media forums for the purposes of changing attitude of those who write, and present Africa in the U.S. media. UCLA, DTM and SAREAT could jointly coordinate such workshops both in the U.S and in East Africa, because African journalists' approach to the continental issues also needs to be changed.

SESSION SIX: PRESENTATION BY KITUO CHA KATIBA - THE EAST AFRICAN CENTRE FOR CONSTITUTIONAL DEVELOPMENT (EACODEV)

Presenter: **Ms. Harriet Busingye,** *Acting Director, ECODEV*
Rapporteur: **Mr. Sabiti Makara,** *Makerere University*

Ms. Busingye outlined the project objectives as:

1. To advance the science, the processes and art of constitution making.
2. To promote the values of constitutionalism, gender equality and equity throughout the East African region.
3. To address the plight of the socially, culturally and economically disadvantaged; culturally and economically disadvantaged groups including, refugees, minorities and people with disabilities.
4. To commission state of the art studies on constitutionalism.

5. To collect and compile memories on prominent East Africans involved in the processes of evolving constitutionalism in the region.
6. To encourage, support and facilitate reforms in school and university curricula to incorporate aspects of constitutionalism.
7. To build a data bank, undertake research, publish and disseminate findings.

The presenter said that for a number of reasons, the project was only able to take off in March 1998. That a Secretariat had been opened in Kampala, Uganda and liaison officers had been identified in Kenya and Tanzania.

The EACODEV had been registered in Uganda and stakeholder had been identified. However, stakeholders are yet to be identified in Kenya and Tanzania.

The EACODEV had taken off with a workshop held in August 1998 at Entebbe, Uganda. The second workshop is planned to take place in November and these seminars is to generate debate on constitutional issues in the region. It is also planned that the EACODEV will soon have a web page on the Internet. It is hoped that the web page will increase synergy among the stakeholders.

During the discussions the following issues emerged:

- First, that the project seems to be having too many objectives, hence the need to prioritise.
- Secondly, it was noted that the project activities seem not to be linked to rural people. It was argued that failure to reach the rural people on issues like land, poverty, ethnicity etc. left the project to the elite.
- The third issue that emerged is whether or not, EACODEV is an advocacy organization. It was clearly clarified that EACODEV was purely a forum for all stakeholders with varying interests.

In response to the above issues, it was generally agreed that EACODEV has no inclination towards a particular group, least it ceases to be a champion of all interests.

On the point of why it took too long for EACODEV to take off, one well informed participant cautioned that it takes sometime to get things in place and that some people like to raise criticisms rather than suggesting solutions. It was further suggested that this workshop should do exactly that. For example, it was suggested that this workshop should lay strategies for learning regional experiences.

Some of the strategies suggested include:

- That EACODEV should not duplicate what other organizations are already doing.
- That stakeholders should take a more active role in shaping the future directions of the organization.
- That issues in each country are different from those in others. So issues pertinent in each country should be identified and be dealt with specifically.

In conclusion, the participants concurred that EACODEV was very relevant and desirable in the wake of the proposal to revive the East African Community and in view of the serious constitutional and political reforms taking place in the region. That although implementation of the project had been delayed, it should be given support to grow.

SESSION SEVEN: PRESENTATION BY DEVELOPMENT THROUGH MEDIA (DTM)

Chairperson: **Ms. Helen Kijo Bisimaba,** *Legal and Human Rights Centre, Dar es Salaam, Tanzania*

Rapporteur: **Ms. Juliet Bintu,** *Faculty of Social Sciences, Makerere University*

Presenter: **Ms. Dommie Yambo-Odotte,** *Development Through Media (DTM)*

Ms. Dommie Yambo-Odotte, Producer and Director of Development Through Media (DTM) reported on her on-going film project, FORGOTTEN. She updated the participants about what has been happening at the DTM regarding the FOREGOTTEN film.

She reminded the participants that for the last one year the research passed through several stages of development. FOREGOTTEN, a story which is basically about women and children in several African countries who were associated with the struggle against apartheid but who now find themselves on the opposite side of the success story.

Issues addressed in the film are outlined as: Issues of Love, and betrayal, betrayal by one's country, betrayal by a movement. It is a human story.
It questions the rights to association of freedom fighters, identity issues of children and women issues.

Since October last year, it was reported that several activities were carried out which included:

a) Further research and data cross-checking where African countries other than South Africa are brought in together with other African people all traced from a historical perspective. It is hoped that the story will inform the on-going political liberation and democratization in East Africa and in particular inform the New South Africa to address its historical mistakes and violations on women and children.

b) Second activity was screening the Play. Participants were also informed that so far four official and almost ten unofficial drafts have been written. Each of the four official drafts have undergone critical sessions involving creative team as well as other selected people including members of the diplomatic corp. The comments from the audience were encouraging and will only help them to improve the script to make a very significant impact in awareness creation.

c) Third activity will include a screen Play. Reaching scheduled for 9th October 1998. This will be followed by a viewing process on 15th October 1998. This stage is followed by production and release which will be ready by 25th February 1999.

Future Direction: Vision and Sustainability

This based on strategic distribution planning for the film to reach targeted audience through out Africa and the rest of the world in general. This requires research and effective information dissemination to the civil society through audio video media using the mushrooming media and broadcasting establishments.

Sustainability

DTM hopes to raise funds from sales and distributor rights which will in turn be re-invested into the production of other audio visual products.

This will be followed by a five year development plan to give a clear picture of the future and sustainability.

Synergy Strategies

The DTM through monthly radio and TV programmes called East Africa Today together with SAREAT's Newsletter will help DTM. They also hope to create training opportunity and publications for future film makers. They will count themselves to more entertaining and educative film.

DISCUSSION

Most participants applauded for the work of DTM and congratulated DTM for the good work in one year. It was reported that already the news of the film have reached South African papers and is already causing an impact in South Africa.

Earlier Ms. Assumpta had briefed participants on how the film was received in Ohio when she presented a paper on the FORGOTTEN. She said the American audiences were very excited about the film and they are looking forward for its release.

There was also a view that the film will be relevant in other crisis places like the Democratic Republic of Congo and Rwanda. There was also a question as to whether there will be a book written for those who will not have a chance of watching the film. Moreover, a question was raised on whether there were strategies to offset negative influences in the film and as to why the film should exclude countries like Ethiopia that trained Mandela.

Dommie answered some of the questions by replying that not everything can be included at the same time but added that the film content is actually African and that the project is about the civil society.

SESSION EIGHT: CREATING SYNERGY – STRATEGIES FOR COLLABORATIVE ACTION FOR THE NEW AFRICA INITIATIVE

Chairperson: **Professor Rwekaza Mukandala,** *Uongozi School, Tanzania*

Speakers: **Prof. Jonathan Moyo,** *University of Witwatersrand, South Africa*
Prof. Pearl Robinson, *Tufts University, USA*

This Session focused on how to create synergy among the Initiative partners. Synergy that strategically promotes dialogue and identifies issues that move NAI forward. The critical challenge for NAI partners was in the re-examination of the common objectives and from that analysis begin to set a course forward into a future that realizes the agenda being formulated today in East Africa. Both Prof. Moyo's and Dr. Robinson's speech articulated these aspects for such synergy and the need for a new vision for Africa through the East African eyes.

Prof. Moyo, "Creating Synergy – New Africa Initiative (NAI) Programs"

Prof. Moyo told the group he was only going to make some observations, since his talk the previous day addressed the subject he was to speak on. He also told the participants that Dr. Robinson had agreed to speak on some relevant issues pertinent to the Initiative.

Prof. Moyo first observations was based on his understanding of what the partners were doing, and his own thinking about the whole question of synergy between the different components of the Initiative. He thought the time had come for the group to have dialogue that was 'strategic'. Strategic in the sense of how different components relate and work with one another. In so doing, he noted meaningful dialogue on the real questions that could emerge. Prof. Moyo advised the group to seriously begin to look beyond the issues of common donor or common funding, and begin to define issues, which enhance the building of partnership. He challenged the participants to take a step back and ask themselves why they were really there. "Are we here because there was an opportunity created by Ford Foundation purely on funding basis? he asked. "Or are we here because, there are certain fundamental questions that pre-occupy our attention, as professionals, as leaders in our respectful organizations, as individuals, as citizen, and if there are those questions, and if so, he asked, "what are they?". Such questions once put forward, he suggested would generate more debate on how to move forward. A dialogue of such nature would further strengthen the NAI.

He then moved on to what he said seemed to be a pending question, the definition of the region itself. "Having sat through meetings for the last two and half years", Prof. Moyo said there was still a disagreement among the participants on the definition of East Africa. Until this was clarified, he said, it would be very difficult to have meaningful dialogue. So, he offered clarity on the subject by saying; "the region East Africa in the case of this Initiative; is East Africa proper, the three East African countries, which share a common geographical and a common history." East Africa within the larger context of Africa, he said represents the birth place for the liberation movements. The lands of Jomo Kenyatta, the lands of Julius Nyerere and in fact the place perhaps, the one-party state was craft especially in Tanzania. If these countries, were moving away from the old model of nation building in Africa, he noted. It is instructive to us, especially the new countries of Southern Africa, to find out exactly what is it, that is causing a re-examination of the fundamental tendency of African nationalism and nation-building, as we have known it for the past 30 years.

In analyzing the changing trend in East Africa from the point of view of those outside the region was the whole question of who is an African, as currently debated in South Africa, (Refer to eight points in Prof. Moyo's speech of October 5, 1998 to NAI). A point Prof. Moyo raised as significant to the Initiative. "Because we cannot be talking about this new Africa without having the notion of what kind of image of individual, we have in mind. There have been assumptions in the past about the definition of an African. I think right now that definition is being challenged because if there is a new Africa perhaps there is also an emerging definition of a new African." Dr. Moyo then elaborated further on the question of who is an African as he raised the debate in the past, which he said had been problematic. As he made reference to the whites in South Africa who used to talk about Afrikaaners, then Africans. Today, the blacks in South Africa are also talking about Africans and South Africans. He then continued on to the situation in the Sudan, "where an Arab minority is oppressing an African majority or the black majority. What is going on there, who is an African, and who is not an African? You've a situation where a lot of people who have claimed to be Africans and have sought the participation in the Organization of African Unity, in fact don't conduct themselves in a way that promotes an image of an emerging kind of an African that people would like people to see".

"I don't think there are obvious answers," he said. "But I think there are uncomfortable questions, I think that there are uncomfortable issues, which we must honestly deal with and not be ashamed of, and not think that by raising these questions, we are creating more problems." This debate he said had a Pan-African element to it. "I think that whereas thirty years ago, we saw the beginnings of a Pan-Africanism that was informed by responses to colonialism, imperialism and slavery. We are today seeing new forms of Pan-Africanism that is responding to different questions, and no longer informed by those kinds of questions that were on the agenda 30 years ago. It is partly informed by responses to leadership corruption, distortions of culture and identity. Corruption of the state itself, marginalization of all kinds of groups and identities, and the new global economic situation, the so-called 'globalization'. We are responding to this, and as we respond to this, we are creating new identities. Sometimes because of historical factors, sometimes because of language factors, but at the end of the day, I think that we are somehow talking about a new Africa because we are in search of new

identities, new Pan-Africanism. Not only as Africans in our regions and the continent, but as people in a new world.
But this, he said, would not be meaningful unless "we understand our own concrete situations. Because there is a lot we know about this region and if we can unravel some of the issues that have become a problem in this region, especially in sub-saharan Africa. I think that the questions therefore you are facing at the end of the day are two: 1) What kind of pan-Africanism are you forging through the NAI as East Africans? 2) What are some of the opportunities that you have given the changing circumstance in the world and what are some of the problems. I think that you have more opportunities than problems; I also think that those opportunities will not be immediately obvious, unless you are willing to deal with the uncomfortable questions and be realistic about those same questions.

Thank you.

Prof. Robinson, "The Way Forward for New Africa Initiative"

Well, if I had known that Jonathan was going to be so magisterial, I would have gone first because this really is a very hard act to follow.

I am going to use the time that was given to me to make suggestions and share my thoughts about synergy, as I have sat here listening to the discussions. As someone who is not part of any of these projects on the table, yet as someone who benefited from the opportunity to spend last year at Makerere University in Uganda, which was a learning experience for me in a number of ways. For the people who know me, I spent my career in Francophone West Africa. So, being in Uganda, being in this region was new for me in a number of ways and I tend to look at things comparatively and I have been absolutely delighted and fascinated by having the opportunity to see it develop.

Let me just begin, first of all by the comment, I made about the 'Way Forward', as I look at and as I teach about African politics. I see, three major paradigms that have sort of shifted in the ways which people have taught about, thought about, and tried to understand and explain Africa. The first paradigms being the paradigm of nationalism and nation building, which was the dominant paradigm when I started studying Africa as an undergraduate, and then as a graduate student. We moved into the period when crisis was the paradigm. I can still remember being in an African Studies Association meeting, I think it may have been, I don't remember where it was now, it was when I met Baregu, who was still a graduate student at Stanford and he said:

'all these pals'. Everybody is talking about Crisis! Crisis! Crisis! And that sort of identified for me the period in which crisis was the paradigm.

What I am struck by, is over the past years....the new paradigm is the Way Forward, that people are talking about Africa not in the nation building model, not in the crisis model. But even when people are talking about crisis, it is framed in trying to understand how do we move forward. We no longer try to assume that Africa is marred and stuck in this crisis phase and there is nothing that can be done to get out. I find that very exciting. I am excited by what I call the way forward paradigm, which has been given the name in the NAI. Every single one of this project, I think is oriented by a desire to understand, to analyze and to point to a way forward. I think Jonathan Moyo has very insightfully pointed out in the work he is doing----that is he is connecting the shift in paradigm to a process of inter-generational change.

There is a new Africa being made by new Africans who have been socialized in the post nationalist period. They have sort of come on the scene, tried to make sense of life and its purposes in the phase of crisis and these people may not be the majority. In the African-American parallel, a talented tenth of these people, have benefit from some extra-ordinary opportunities. They have had to both develop professional competencies, insights, network beyond their own countries. They have benefited from an opportunity that has made them begin to say, we don't have to spend the rest of our lives, and our children don't have to be condemned to this phase of crisis.

For me, the NAI is not about East Africa. The NAI is something I walked into based on my experience in West Africa. I must also say, based on my experience as an African-American, dealing both as an academic, where I deal with multiple generations, as an activist, where I am involved with people of my own generations, generations in front of me, and generations behind. In which, we too are trying to find a way forward. When I look at my friends, my activist phase of my life, I also see a new pan-Africanism. I have never articulated this in paper, but verbally, I have shared my thoughts with people on this. At some point, I am going to write about pan-Africanism, as I see it in African-American, but I do think, that is all relate to what we are doing here. So, the NAI has it own East African specificity, and I think that is what people grapple with here, and you should not expect to be able to do it in two or three meetings.

Synergy for me means making the connections initially with these projects. We all in this room, are brought together by the Ford Foundation because it is funding the projects. First of all, you've to figure out what are the connections among these projects. You must think about that with the understanding of what synergy means. And this is going to spill over to lots of other arenas, in your own countries, in the neighboring countries in West Africa, with what is going on in the United States, in what is happening with other people who are trying to identify new pan-Africanisms. Synergy for me means connection, cross-learning across your own sub area in which you work, across your own country and your own discipline. As I was listening to the presentation of DTM, I think it is a wonderful example of synergy in ways that are not necessary self-evident but somehow jumps at me, that this is what is really about. First having read the treatment, I haven't read the screen play itself, but in reading the treatment, it is very clear what I think about this project. It is trans-generational. The fact that we look at a problem in the anti-apartheid struggle, and we see it from the perspective of a generation of children, that is a generation who are a product of this struggle. And so, there is a connection in the film with all of these projects, which ought to have on its agenda, a trans-generational slice based on what you are doing. So, constitutional reform project, which I think has a number of serious problems is very important for one not to think of it not only in the context of what is happening in these three countries to-day, but also as a trans-generational slice.

Another thing about the film project is, it forces us to think about how to communicate a message in a discourse that will appeal to the audiences we are trying to reach. Dommie articulated that as the top agenda, on what you have to do when you are making a film. I think every single one of this project needs to do that, and that is something that you can learn from just listening to the way in which she describe the work that she is doing. It is a mind set that ought to be infused in all of these projects. It was interesting that this is a film, not a film that is simply a documentary but aims at a mass media. I think everyone of these projects in some way specific to whatever it is that you are doing, you should ask the question, how can I, aim at a mass media and how big is this audience that I may be able to attract.

SAREAT, I think is a project that is of profound importance as part of the glue of these project, and I have said this in our discussions. I think at least from my perspective having lived in Uganda, it looks to me to be too focused on Kenya. You must have some one token thing that you are doing that is going to be visible, that is going to have a spread effect in Uganda, in Tanzania. And from the beginning, these other projects feel there is a connection, and that you can perform that role of glue, which I think is so essential and I think you can build the structure.

The NMK project, how do you make this work and how do you make it accessible? It is not just the material, that I am hopeful we can figure a way to get the images digitized, so I can work them into a web-site, that I hope to develop for a course that I am teaching. I might say, a course that I hope to co-develop with a couple of universities in the region. What I was struck by in your presentation was, it was not just the specifics that you are doing, but about an idea on how to talk about and think about culture. I was one of the people who sat on the selection of some of the students, who went to Uongozi, and some of the discussion we had was about culture. I made notes for myself, and I had something to do with the curriculum with Uongozi. I was struck by many of the students who saw culture as something in the past, and when do you get women more involved, people said you've to overcome African culture. The idea how one understands culture and tradition is one that needs to be fused into all of these projects, and that to me may be in fact your most important contribution. So, it is not just about having a museum exhibit, and making things available on the internet, but a way of thinking about culture that needs to orient all these projects.

The Uongozi Institute, I think is one of the important projects, specifically because it is a sort of foundation that is orienting the leadership of a new Africa. When, I look at Uongozi, I think about the organization that preceded the US Peace Corp. It was called Cross Roads Africa, started actually by an African-American minister, whose name was Robinson, no relation as far as I can figure. The idea that he had was to send young American students to Africa, and have them work with their African age-mates in community, where they built something together. They would build a school, they would build a community center, and they would build road. The idea being, at this critical formative age in the lives of young people, young people who were destined and he knew that the sort of people who would opt to do this, these are people who were destined to be future leaders. Later on when Kennedy became president, he took that as a model for the peace corp. People who are today in their 50s, who were in that first generation of CrossRoaders both in Africa and the United States are in fact leaders. They had experiences that enable them to make contributions to their own societies.

Let me just finish by saying that, one of the ways, I benefited from spending a year in Uganda; I also benefited in so many ways even in my physical and mental health. I am in the process of writing a chapter in a book that is doing a comparative history of area studies in the United States, and I am writing the Africa chapter. And sitting in Uganda and thinking about the NAI, and thinking about lots of things, I decided to conceptualize my chapter by talking about three worlds of African studies. When people talk about American universities, where they have centers for African studies, area of study of other parts of the world, like the African Studies Center at UCLA, my own university does not have one of these centers. So, I looked at that world with a sort of slightly different task. I originally agreed to write this chapter because I wanted to write into that history, the history of African studies at historically black colleges in the United States.

In fact, the very first African studies course were introduced at America university at historically black colleges in the last century, where these institutions felt it was important as part of what meant to be a well educated African-American, to know something about Africa. And then, when the big African Studies centers were created by the foundations, they past over that world, so people generally ignore that phase. I agreed to write this because I wanted to write about the African-American black into the study of African studies. But over here, I realized there was another world that frequently is not talked about when people talk about area studies in the United States, or specifically when people talk about African Studies. And that is the world of African universities and institutions where people are doing on the ground fundamental work of African studies. I think that African researchers spend so much time in acknowledging what research institution and sort of higher education in the United States, and Europe are doing the sort of agenda setting work that was being ignoring by you. So, what I am trying to do, is to write a piece that will talk about three worlds of African studies, Europe is not on my article cause that was not my assignment. I am writing about; the world of African studies at major US research institutions, the world of African studies at historically black colleges and the world of African studies at African universities and research institutions. I am going to argue that there is intellectual, and intellectual agendas in all of these three worlds that the world frequently operates as though the other two don't exist, or in some way subservient to the US Research University. But the fact is that Africa as a continent, Africans as a people would be better off, if we could get synergy from these three worlds, acknowledging their existence and thinking about how, they relate to each other, and try to get all these three worlds involved in the 'Way Forward'.

DISCUSSION

The question of inclusion of Ethiopia dominated the discussions, as the colleagues from Ethiopian felt need for their inclusion.

Both issues raised in the speeches about the new African and the need for the way forward. It was suggested that the way forward could not be found unless a new definition of a new African was found. It seemed apparent that the project by NMK offered some answers, but more was done into the past culture to find that definition of a new Africa. An African, as was suggested, who would understand constitutions and constitutionalism. But this would only come about with Africans changing their own attitude about themselves, by understanding what they were all about.

As the discussions continued, participants pondered over the way forward, others posed the question of relevance. How to really locate the NAI within the context of what was going in East Africa, on the whole continent and globally. It was therefore felt that the NAI ought to relate to what was going on in society. To achieve this, it was suggested that the Initiative had to find a direct link with struggles relating to democratic questions, questions about Africa's role in the international economic system, and unless that was done, the NAI could remain academic.

CONCLUDING SESSION

Dr. Tegegne Teka, the Facilitator of the Workshop

Dr. T. Teka, made the following remarks in the Closing Session. He said that on behalf of OSSREA and on his behalf, he would like to thank everybody for coming here given the tight schedule you are all engaged in. We benefited from what you contributed. OSSREA will try to use your suggestions, recommendations, and ideas to work for better results. As you all know, OSSREA is of course a regional organization; we have been working for Africa and we are a Pan-African organization. The spirit in which we are working is to serve the region and the continent, institutions and individuals. OSSREA's mandate is indeed much broader, it is World peace and order. In fact, we listened attentively to much of what most of you have said, and we have recorded that. We will continue to improve on our performance.

We are happy that the NAI is working at the grassroots. We are also happy that we work together with Initiatives that reflect grassroots environment. We are ready to continue to work with individuals and institutions that demand our support and our help. Come as individuals or come as organizations, we are here to promote social research and understanding between peoples. OSSREA would try to look into avenues of generating funds to work closer with you and others to achieving NAI objectives. I wish you a safe journey back. I thank you very much for coming and for your contributions. Thank you very much.

Dr. Mukandala, Chairperson

Dr. Mukandala, thanked Dr. Teka, who spoke as facilitator of the workshop and representative of OSSREA. He also said that on behalf of member organizations and members of the NAI, he thanked each and every member of the Workshop participants who took their time to have come flying thousands of miles to attend this important workshop. We have benefited very greatly, and for Uongozi, speaking as Uongozi person, I know we have benefited a lot from your suggestions. We have been stimulated by the ideas that have been thrown around, talk of new paradigms, etc. of a new Africa. I find it was very interesting and worth the time of coming here. I am sure other projects have also learnt from you and also from each other, and have been able to compare themselves to other projects and what it is they can do better. But of course, we also met old friends, whom we have not met for a while, and also new people and hopeful we have made new friends. But in the final analysis, I hope we had a very honest and committed and truthful discussion and contribution, everything that was said was for the betterment and improvement of what it is that we want to achieve. It is nothing personal, so please leave this room feeling very happy and that you are all valued personally and for your ideas.

As it was mentioned by my predecessor Dr. Isakahia, we have decided that we are going to have this informal coordination of the NAI Steering Committee. We will try this time to be more active and we will try to take up the challenge of raising funds as has been mentioned, to make sure we have this kind of gathering next year. So with those words, I would like to thank you all for coming and then declare this workshop closed.

2

NEW AFRICA INITIATIVE

Jonathan N. Moyo[*]

1. Introduction

Over the past decade, and especially the last six years, Kenya, Uganda and Tanzania have gone through major social, political and economic ferment. The repeal of Section 2(a) of the Kenyan Constitution in December 1991 ended one party rule culminating in a spirited competition for political power. In 1988 Uganda started an impressive constitution-making process which reached a milestone in March 1994 when Ugandans elected a Constituent Assembly which openly debated and eventually promulgated a new democratic constitution in October 1995. Tanzania abandoned its socialist claims used to justify monopoly politics and adopted political pluralism in 1993 leading to the country's first multi-party general election in October and November 1995. These developments were given further momentum in 1996 by the revival of economic and political co-operation among the three East African countries under the co-ordination of the East African Co-operation Secretariat re-established in Arusha, Tanzania. The three East African countries are now experiencing a historic up-tide in plural politics. While this up-tide has led to new opportunities for deepening and broadening democratization in East Africa, concomitant needs have emerged as a result of two important considerations.

First, the activism and ideas behind the changes in favor of democracy in East Africa have remained a preserve of elite groups: bureaucrats, political parties, academics, NG0s and the donor community. Second, and because of the first reason, the dissemination of information and ideas about the changes that are either taking place or are proposed is often done in esoteric publications, seminars and workshops that are not accessible to ordinary East Africans. Consequently, there is a growing gap between the demands for democratic

[*] Program Officer, Governance and Civil Society Program, Ford Foundation, Eastern Africa Office, Nairobi, Kenya.

changes being made by the elite groups and popular perceptions of the changes sought. This has raised the risk that ordinary East Africans are going to become cynical about the process of democratic transitions in the region. As a response to this risk, the Ford Foundation's Governance and Civil Society Program for Eastern Africa launched the "New Africa Initiative" in Entebbe, Uganda, at a workshop held from July 15 to 18, 1996. The workshop was attended by 54 prominent East Africans and international resource persons working on issues of democratisation and human rights in East Africa.

2. The Initiative

The New Africa Initiative targets the next generation of East Africans with the ultimate objective of fostering democratic constitutionalism and good governance in the region. In this connection, the Initiative seeks to promote the cultivation of a democratic public mind-set and to engender mutually beneficial interaction among key governmental, civil society and knowledge-generating institutions and individuals. To achieve this objective, the Initiative seeks to: (1) generate policy-relevant knowledge by identifying and supporting the next generation of East African leaders at key universities and research institutes in the region; (2) promote democratic constitution-making through a regionally co-ordinated institutional effort and (3) promote democratic social mobilization through alternative research, film, public debate, scholarly and popular publication of governance ideas.

3. Objectives of the Initiative

More specifically, the Initiative's interim objectives are: (1) to establish an East African "summer" school as an intellectual forum to break down old barriers between policy-makers and academia and to forge new linkages among the next generation of leaders in Eastern Africa and their peers in North America and elsewhere; (2) to establish a regional center to promote constitutional development in Eastern Africa as an issue of importance to everyday life beyond the event of constitution-writing; (3) to establish publication series on emerging East African alternatives to communicate innovative governance and policy ideas to the next generation of East Africans in politics, education, the civil service, business, and the growing non-profit sector; (4) to bring critical ideas on the governance debate in Eastern Africa from elite individuals and groups to the level of ordinary East Africans through film and (5) to promote partnerships between local communities and key governmental institutions through research and policy action to revive traditional knowledge on conflict resolution and democratic governance within a modern context. These objectives will be pursued by six organizations working in East Africa - Kituo cha Katiba (in Kiswahili), Uongozi School (in Kiswahili), Series on Alternative Research in East Africa (SAREAT), National Museums of Kenya (NMK), Development Through Media (DTM), and Organization for Social Science Research in Eastern and Southern Africa (OSSREA). [Figure 1, p. 47]

4. Kituo cha Katiba

Kituo cha Katiba's primary mission is to stimulate multi and inter-disciplinary dialogue and action on constitution-making, constitutionalism and democratic governance in Eastern Africa. This will be done through basic and applied research, information dissemination and public debate. Of particular concern will be the development of programs of constitutional advocacy and activism, policy-formulation and advice, technical assistance within the region, and constitutional reform and revision. The Center will target various levels of East African society including the government, civil society, academia, the arts, the professions, and especially the next generation.

The project leaders have concluded that constitution-making is not the end of the process but just the beginning. The larger and more important issue is one of building a viable political community in the long run: a state that generates governance by consent under the rule of law leading to democratic civil society. To this end, the project will promote regional consensus around the need for a non-partisan institution that will have the credibility to foster a wider and deeper discussion of constitutional development in Eastern Africa.

Conceived as a project that will complement rather than supplant current national efforts in the three East African countries, Kituo cha Katiba will seek linkages and collaboration with existing projects and institutions within and beyond Eastern Africa. The Center will pay particular attention to information collection, research and public debate of constitutional issues of a pan-East African nature. The Center will create a network of organizations and individuals committed to the ideals of constitutional development within and across the three East African countries.

The objectives of Kituo cha Katiba are:

- To advance the science, processes and art of constitution-making, constitutionalism and democratic governance in Eastern Africa through basic, comparative and applied research;
- To commission state of the art studies on various dimensions of constitution-making;

- To promote the values and ethos of constitutionalism and gender equality and equity;
- To address the plight of disadvantaged social, cultural, economic and political groups in Eastern Africa, including minorities, refugees and people with disabilities;
- To collect and compile the testimonies of prominent East Africans who are involved in the processes of constitutional evolution and development in Eastern Africa; and to foster the contribution of grassroots operatives to these processes;
- To host an annual public lecture by a prominent East African on constitutional development in the region; and to widely disseminate the text of the lecture to diverse audiences in and outside the region;
- To create and maintain a directory of individuals and institutions committed to democratic constitutionalism in Eastern Africa;
- To encourage, support and facilitate the reform of school and university curricula incorporating important issues of constitution-making, constitutionalism and democratic governance;
- To act as a regional watchdog for the protection, promotion and enhancement of constitution-making, constitutionalism and democratic governance; and
- To foster solidarity with local, national, regional and international organizations;

The Nairobi office of the Ford Foundation believes that Kituo cha Katiba will fill the gap in the institutional landscape of an emerging new Eastern Africa. Currently, there is no regional body dealing with the important issues identified by the Center. Yet the region is increasingly asserting itself as a community. The center is therefore timely and its program is innovative.

5. Uongozi School

The "Uongozi School" (Uongozi is a Kiswahili word for "leadership") will be based in Arusha, Tanzania under the auspices of the University of Dar es Salaam. The preparatory work for the school was co-ordinated by the Organization for Social Science Research in Eastern and Southern Africa (OSSREA) and led by a working group comprising of Professor Rwekaza S. Mukandala, (the co-ordinator of the group from the University of Dar es Salaam), Professor Joseph O. Nyunya (University of Nairobi), Professor Edmond Keller (University of California at Los Angeles - UCLA), Professor

Foster Byarugaba (Makerere University) and Professor A. S. Kiondo (University of Dar es Salaam).

With a focus and emphasis on economic development issues, community relations, constitutional change and comparative area studies, Uongozi School will cover contemporary research and public policy debates on democratic values and constitutional processes between the state and civil society in the Eastern Africa region along with perspectives from other regions in and outside Africa.

The Uongozi School will be a unique and a path-breaking collaborative project of the four universities under the co-ordination of the University of Dar es Salaam. The involvement of UCLA will enable the James S. Coleman Center for African Studies to contribute to the revitalization of African Studies in the United States with a focus on Eastern Africa. Professor Mukandala and his colleagues believe that there is a need for an intellectual forum to nurture and harness the democratic ideas of the next generation of African leaders in ways that are reminiscent of the various meeting points enjoyed by the early African nationalists such as Jomo Kenyatta, Kwame Nkurumah, Julius Nyerere, Kamuzu Banda and many others who despite their ideological differences, used various fora when they were students to discuss and shape the future of Africa.

The school will have five objectives:

- To support the making of a new East Africa by enhancing the intellectual growth of promising undergraduate students in the region by exposing them to current theoretical, methodological and popular debates in the social sciences, arts, law, NGO, state and civil society;
- To enable the students apply their knowledge to critical analysis of concrete socio-economic and constitutional problems in their home countries and the Eastern Africa region;
- To provide a forum for an intensive exchange of research and innovative ideas, under the supervision and with the participation of leading scholars, activists and policy makers, on the periodically selected current topics;
- To train students as future leaders in their home countries and the Eastern Africa region by exposing them to the interdependence of the region arising from the historical and emerging political and economic realities of the three East African countries and their neighbors; and
- To develop an internship program for the students as a bridge between theory and practice.

The Nairobi Office of the Ford Foundation is very encouraged by this initiative, especially because the initiative presents challenging opportunities to the participating universities to forge new linkages, revitalize African Studies and stimulate the imagination of the next generation of East Africans.

6. Series on Alternative Research in East Africa Trust (SAREAT)

The journal and publication initiative will be run by the Series on Alternative Research in East Africa Trust (SAREAT). Based in Nairobi, and led by Mutahi Ngunyi, one of Eastern Africa's most promising scholars belonging to the younger generation, SAREAT is a recently established research and publication forum to communicate innovative governance ideas to the next generation of East Africans in education, the civil service, commerce and industry and the growing non-profit sector. This will be done through the publication of a monthly journal and books and the hosting of regional monthly public meetings on the policy implications of democratic transitions in Eastern Africa. The initiative will give emerging East African scholars, policy analysts and practitioners a regular forum for disseminating new concepts to shape democratic governance in the region. There is no other regional forum of this kind in Eastern Africa.

The establishment of SAREAT is, therefore, a welcome development which is consistent with the Ford Foundation's objective to promote democratic values through open debate and dialogue.

7. National Museums of Kenya (NMK)

The Museums Trustees of Kenya have established a policy project to enable the National Museums of Kenya (NMK) to promote partnerships between local communities and governmental agencies to revive traditional knowledge on democracy and conflict resolution in Kenya today. Led by NMK's Director General, Dr. Mohammed Isahakia, the project will use Kenya's national museums as a forum to revisit and critically discuss the values and institutions of traditional East Africa as a means for promoting cross-cultural understanding and pluralism within the modern context of democratic governance.

NMK's regional museums will be the focal points for building inter-group cultural dialogues to promote understanding and harmony among Kenya's diverse ethnic groups. This will be an important contribution to the current governance debate in Eastern Africa in view of the growing number of ethnic voices demanding a stake in the constitution-making process throughout the region. NMK's proposal is particularly attractive because it places a major Kenyan institution with regional influence in Eastern Africa into a new role in which it addresses the often noted but little acted upon need for promoting positive mutual images among Kenya's many diverse ethnic groups.

NMK's thesis is that ethnicity, which is an African reality, can be seen as a resource for building sustainable political and socio-economic development from within. The proposed project will test this thesis. In that connection, the project is a useful addition to the New Africa Initiative not only because it addresses the all important question of the future of ethnicity in a democratic Eastern Africa but also because it targets ordinary citizens.

8. Development Through Media (DTM)

The media initiative to popularize governance ideas in East Africa among ordinary people will be run by a media-NGO, Development Through Media (DTM), which is working on a docudrama film under the title, "The Forgotten Lot". The setting of the story is based on the connection of ordinary East Africans (mainly Tanzanians but also Kenyans and Ugandans) with the New South Africa. Many East Africans, indeed the rest of the world, have forgotten about the sacrifices made by ordinary Tanzanians, through public protest and associational life, to the end of apartheid in South Africa. In a significant but so far unrecognized way, the sacrifices and public protests were and remain a part and parcel of the struggle for democracy and good governance in Tanzania in particular, and East Africa in general. But all that has been forgotten, hence the title of the film: ***The Forgotten Lot.***

Led by Dommie Yambo-Odotte, the highly respected and committed Kenyan female film producer who has won international awards for her outstanding work, DTM was formed and registered in 1996 as a non-profit media public company based in Nairobi, Kenya. DTM, which is the only organization of its kind in Kenya, seeks to use film as a tool for transforming the public mind-set in East Africa from an authoritarian to a democratic orientation. Ms. Yambo-Odotte and her colleagues at DTM believe that the media, especially the use of docudrama on film, has prodigious impact as a tool for popularizing important governance ideas among ordinary people who otherwise have no access to specialized sources of information or esoteric debate in the political process. DTM's assessment of the lopsided nature of information dissemination in Eastern Africa is shared by the Foundation's staff in the Nairobi office who have previously explored various ways of using film to reach wide and diverse audiences of ordinary East Africans to advance values and ideas which support democratic governance. DTM's project is a central component of the Foundation's New Africa Initiative, especially the part which seeks to extend the governance debate in Eastern Africa from elite circles to ordinary people through the mass media.

9. Organization for Social Science Research in Eastern and Southern Africa (OSSREA)

OSSREA played a midwifery role in launching the core activities of the New Africa Initiative, particularly through a meeting in Addis Ababa, Ethiopia, in February 1996 that focused on the concept of the "summer" school and through a later meeting in Entebbe, Uganda, in July 1997 which focused on the core activities of the New Africa Initiative. OSSREA staff collaborated with the working groups that emerged from the Entebbe meeting whose work has led to the five activities presented above. OSSREA is well placed to contribute to the New Africa Initiative by creating a forum for the core programs in the Initiative to communicate with each other and to work for synergy.

OSSREA will link the major partners in the New Africa Initiative with universities and social scientists in eastern and southern Africa through its well established networks and name recognition. In effect, OSSREA will provide a useful glue to the New Africa Initiative. Under the guidance of its regional co-ordinator, Dr. Tegegne Teka, the workshops will have the following specific objectives:

- To further advance the goals of the New Africa Initiative;
- To provide a forum for critical evaluation of the activities of programs under the New Africa Initiative;
- To refine and identify further areas of collaboration among key partners in the New Africa Initiative and other initiatives in and outside Eastern Africa;
- To explore existing and possible strategies through which the New Africa Initiative could have wider and deeper impact in Eastern Africa;
- To provide partners in the New Africa Initiative with comparative experience;
- To examine other relevant issues to enhance the individual and collective purposes of the partners in the New Africa Initiative; and

- To identify fund-raising strategies and sources to promote the long-term sustainability of the joint programs under the New Africa Initiative.

10. The Ford Foundation

Ford Foundation programming in Eastern Africa is conducted by its Representative and Program Officers and an administrative staff who are based in Nairobi, Kenya.

Significant and durable social progress in Eastern Africa will come from the efforts of many actors, including government agencies, non-governmental organizations, community-based organizations, universities, private businesses and outside donor organizations. With the limited resources at its disposal, the Foundation supports the strengthening and evolution of local institutions with the capacity to generate and apply new bodies of knowledge. The Foundation makes grants to fund experimentation, learning and demonstration. The principal areas of grant making are Peace and Social Justice, Asset Building and Community Development, Education, Media, Arts and Culture.

Grant from the Foundation addresses **three interconnected issues** in Eastern Africa:

- How to assist the transition in Eastern Africa to a more enabling environment through constitution-making and reform of laws and state structures;
- How to promote value systems, local philanthropy and effective non-state organizations which articulate civil society in Eastern Africa; and
- How to assist the poor and disenfranchised to gain access to justice as well as information, skills and assets they need to empower themselves to improve their lives.

Figure 1: NEW AFRICA INITIATIVE

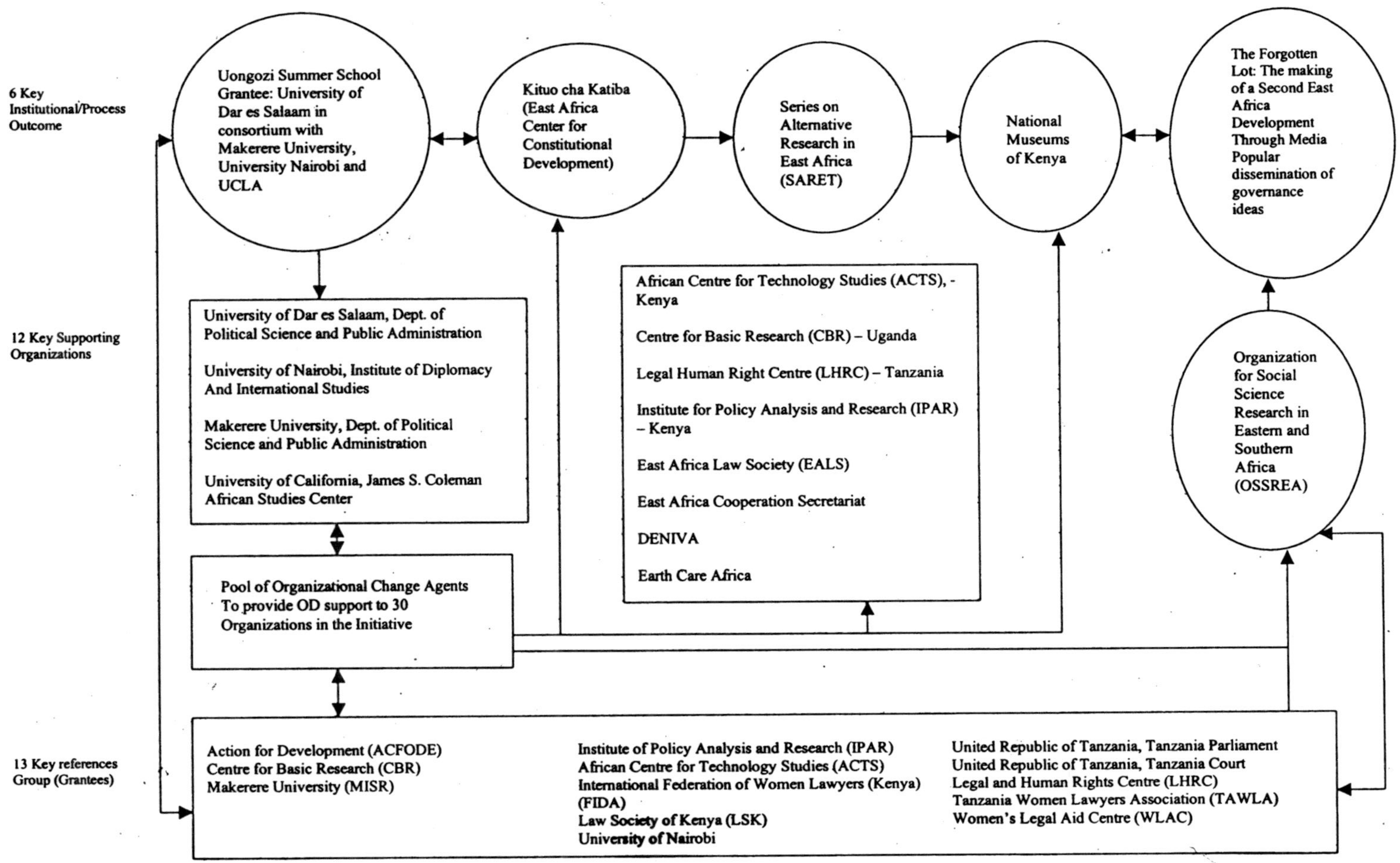

3

KITUO CHA KATIBA: EAST AFRICAN CENTER FOR CONSTITUTIONAL DEVELOPMENT

Harriet Busingye[•]

1. Introduction

East Africa is in a period of tremendous flux and transition, in a fashion perhaps as profound as any since Kenya, Tanganyika and Uganda achieved independence in the early 1960s. Born of the same colonial legacy, and in part the creation of an overriding and irrepressible historical momentum, relations between the three countries have been both turbulent and smooth; co-operative and competitive. One need only think back to the heyday of independence struggles to grasp this sibling rivalry. Imbued with the spirit of *pan-Africanism*, the post-colonial leadership of Julius Nyerere, Jomo Kenyatta and Apollo Milton Obote spoke in eloquent terms of the political union and federation of their three countries. Nyerere was even prepared to delay the formal grant of Tanganyikan independence in order to bring his colleagues on board in a untied East Africa. Ideological division and an element of growing territorialism led to cold feet. Instead, they settled for a loose association of economic interests – the East African Community (EAC) – as the idea of political federation became a more distant dream. Despite being an exemplar of regional co-operation emulated by many others around the world, the Community failed to survive the political differences that plagued the region's leadership and was particularly affected by Idi Amin's unpredictability, the perception of unequal economic gain and a good deal of external manipulation and individual egotism. Sent into cold storage in 1977, it has taken nearly two decades for the subject of co-operation among the three countries to be broached again: once bitten; twice shy!

Today, the winds of change are blowing across East Africa with a momentum that is striking for its pace; there is a fresh impetuous for co-operation abroad,

[•] Acting Director, Kituo Cha Katiba, Kampala, Uganda.

and the peoples of the region are approaching the question from the political, economic, social, and cultural dimensions. Such change and excitement have engulfed both the political leadership (today comprising Benjamin Mkapa in Tanzania, Daniel arap Moi of Kenya, and Uganda's Yoweri Kaguta Museveni) and the various components of civil society in all the three countries. This has prompted the desire to seek closer forms of union and pursue a co-operative approach to the multifarious issues that confront the region as we approach the new millennium.

It is as an integral part of this momentum and with the view to fostering the benefits of regional co-operation that this proposal is being mooted. Consequently, the Working Group on Constitutional Development in East Africa[1] proposes to establish ***Kituo cha Katiba: The East African Centre for Constitutional Development*** (EACODEV). The purpose of EACODEV is to generate a regional institutional framework for the promotion of constitutionalism, constitutional development and democratic governance in East Africa. Drawing from the belief expressed by a cross-section of interested East Africans that such an initiative is particularly necessary at this point in time, EACODEV will promote the creation of an autonomous, pan-regional dialogue and action devoted to the exploitation of the common historical affinities and contemporary experiences of the peoples of the region. It also aims at advancing the pursuit of a more comprehensive understanding of the potential for mutual benefit in and between the three countries.

EACODEV's primary mission is to stimulate a multi and interdisciplinary dialogue on constitution-making, constitutionalism and democratic governance in the East African region. This is to be undertaken through basic and applied research, information dissemination, and public debate. Of particular concern is the development of programs of constitutional advocacy and activism, *amici curiae* briefs for judicial and administrative action; lobbying, policy-formulation and advice; technical assistance within the region, and constitutional reform and revision. EACODEV will target various levels of East African society, including government, civil society, academia, the arts, the professions and the youth. EACODEV shall pay particular attention to information collection, research and the discussion of constitutional issues of a pan-East African nature. Special attention will be lent to the creation of network of organizations and individuals committed to the ideals of constitutional development within the individual countries of the

[1] The Working Group on Constitutional Development in East Africa was estalbished to create a forum for the critical consideraiton and debate of issues relating to the quest for democratic governance and progressive consitutioanlism in the region. The Group held its first meeting in Kampala on October 12 and 13, 1996, out of which broad agreement was reached on the contents of this proposal.

region. In this regard, EACODEV shall support the struggles for the establishment of a truly democratic community in East Africa with thoroughness, objectivity, ideological neutrality and non-alignment.

EACODEV intends to contribute to the dual processes of constitutionalism and constitutional development and regional cooperation that have been underway in East Africa since the late 1980s. It will provide a mechanism and forum for, *inter alia*, the systematic collection and analysis of materials on East African constitutionalism, the collection of the views of prominent actors in the region's independence struggles, and the reform of school and university curricula. Such an approach is prompted by two basic assumptions, *viz:* despite the overall political context of tension, rivalry and individual idiosyncrasies and megalomania, there is an underlying (non-state) comity and affinity between the peoples of the region, and second, the idea of an independent, pan-regional political community which fosters an appreciation of the unique location and opportunities for the countries of East Africa is an idea whose time has now arrived.

This proposal provides a background information on the project and describes the process to be followed as well as the anticipated outcomes of the project. It concludes with a request to meet project start-up and operation costs over a two year cycle. Given the nature of the project envisaged and the scale of activities anticipated, the proposal is being simultaneously circulated to other donors in the quest for consortium funding for the project. The ultimate objective of such a consortium funding would be to pool resources for the raising of an endowment to provide for institutional sustainability.

2. Background

2.1 Conceptual Basis and Rationale

Several concerns informed the process that led to this proposal. The first is that the issue of constitutionalism and constitutional development has been one important concern in East Africa for several years. The concern emerged from the widespread dissatisfaction with the performance of the governments in the region leading to a wanton disrespect for human rights, the lack of accountability to the citizenry, and the prevalence of bad and undemocratic modes of governance. In the wake of the various transitions to different forms of government that have been witnessed in the region since the mid-1980s, increased attention has been placed on the issue of constitutional government. Against such a background, one of EACODEV's primary objectives is to give expression to the need to transcend the individual idiosyncrasies and often megalomaniac posturing of the political leadership, and to simultaneously capture the underlying non-state comity, mutuality of interest and affinity between the peoples of the region. Secondly, we strongly believe that the time for an independent, pan-regional political community which fosters an appreciation of the unique location and opportunities for the countries of East Africa has arrived. Such an initiative must be rooted in a keen respect for the idea of democratic governance and progressive constitutional reform and development.

Following upon two decades of violent non-constitutionalism, economic dislocation and the breakdown of systems of accountability in the case of Uganda, a constitutional-reform exercise was initiated in 1988. The outcomes of this exercise are now enshrined in the 1995 Constitution. The process of constitutional reform generated significant debate about the need for a systemic and transparent approach to government; laid down mechanisms of central and local accountability, and created sufficient checks and balances to executive and/or administrative excess. The 1995 Constitution marks the termination of this debate, and the commencement of a new, and intricately more involved and exciting process: the implementation of the grand ideals contained in the document. In short, the quest for the establishment of a ***culture*** of constitutionalism that transcends lip-service and rhetorical respect for the document. While Uganda's tumultuous history gives cause for a cautious and restrained embrace of the changes that have occurred, the prevailing situation provides some hope that the scope for action has been widened, and that potential exists for enhanced democratic exercise.

In the several decades since each achieved independence, both Kenya and Tanzania have witnessed comparatively more stable government than in the case of Uganda. As in the case of Uganda, both embarked on independence within the broad framework of a Westminster-like model of governance, with secure Bills of Rights, distinct mechanisms to facilitate the separation of powers, and functioning (although micro-national) political parties. These did not last long as the culture of "developmentalism" caught sway and was brought to bear with similar ramifications in both countries despite the distinctiveness of ideologies to which they subscribed. The net result for both Kenya and Tanzania was the single party state. The comparative stability of both countries was essentially negative, in so far as it was couched within the framework of the mechanisms of a one party state which tolerated only minimal dissent. Moreover, those structures cajoled, stifled and barricaded opposition political activity into virtual non-existence. The outcome was that one party controlled political activity, one trade union organized the laboring classes, one women's organization addressed women's concerns, and one youth association dealt with students and their ilk and all were propagandized by one newspaper.

In the wake of global reforms that ushered the collapse of the Berlin Wall, both Kenya and Tanzania distanced themselves from the notion of single-party statehood. In the case of Tanzania it was via the rather circuitous route of a Commission headed by Chief Justice Nyalali. Although initially reluctant, Kenya eventually acceded to growing pressures for multiparty reform through the repeal of Article 2A of its Constitution. Since then, multiparty elections have been held in both countries. If nothing else, those elections reveal in bold relief that despite the formal constitutional transitions, the sceptre of "one-partyism" remains embedded in both the constitutional framework and within the structures of governance that exist in each country today. In short, the quest for genuine pluralism is still elusive and the process of constitutional development has only just commenced.

But the issue of constitutions and constitutionalism is not something simply confined to the geographical parameters of the present proposal; there is a basic conceptual issue at stake too. The African continent has long been involved in the quest for a notion of constitutionalism that is true to its specific identity - an identity that has been characterized by both internal growth and development and external influence and direction. In the early sixties, this found expression in the debate over *autochothony*, manifest in the policies of Africanization, nationalization, and the creation of the ubiquitous parastatal. These experiments collapsed on the seas of the thawing Cold War, the trauma of economic crisis and dislocation, as well as the intrinsically illiberal and undemocratic intentions of those who were behind their design. If there is any lesson to be learnt for the failure of the African experiments in constitutionalism of the 1960s, the effort must emerge from the grassroots, and not be imposed on it. It is to foster such grassroots and indigenous visions of an enduring African constitutionalism that is at the core of the present initiative.

This proposal is also informed by, and relates to, significant developments in the arena of regional cooperation. The three East African countries share an intricate colonial and post-colonial history that spans the social, economic, political and cultural spheres of human existence and organization. That heritage is retraceable to the same impetus of imperial growth and expansion in the region. This partly led to the creation of an irrepressible momentum for closer union and cooperation between them. At the same time, relations between the three have not been smooth, and a sibling rivalry still exists dating back to the heyday of the struggle for independence. That rivalry may explain the failure to create a political union on the attainment of independence, and also throws significant light on the demise of the East African Community in 1977. The wide-scale lamentation for this loss illustrates that the peoples of the region feel an affinity for one another which might not be replicated by its leadership, and which persists despite the often chilly relations between them.

Nevertheless, the process of cooperation between the three countries of the region has witnessed significant growth since the early 1990s. That growth led to the establishment of the Secretariat for East African Cooperation at Arusha, Tanzania. For East Africans with nostalgic (albeit bittersweet) memories of the East African Community, the re-establishment of cooperation was a rekindled dream, the birth of a new regional nirvana. At the same time, it has become abundantly clear that in order to prevent a veritable *dé jà vu*, the process of cooperation must be appropriated and fostered by the citizenry of East Africa, rather than by the dominant political actors in the region. This realization has led to several non-governmental and civil society initiatives in the area, including the East Africa Law Society (EALS), the Women and Law in East Africa (WLEA) Project, and the East African Cooperation Forum (EACF), to mention only a few. Such initiatives need to be applauded, particularly as some of them were pursued and concretized within the teeth of hostile official relations. But more importantly they need to be supported in the bid to create a critical mass of pan-East African institutions and organizations that act as a counter-weight to official hegemony and political control in the region.

The Working Group takes note of the proposal to establish the East African Uongozi (Leadership) Institute and the *Journal of East African Alternatives*. The two initiatives address critical issues that are complementary to the tasks that EACODEV will pursue. It is also intended that there be mutuality of cooperation, operation and regular collaboration on the key issues being addressed by these institutions. As we enter the new millennium, EACODEV intends to fill in the significant lacunae not addressed by these initiatives and to build upon their contribution to the creation of an ethos of "East Africanism." But that ethos must be rooted in concrete notions of constitutional governance and democratic accountability. Such lacunae include the conduct of a systematic, basic, comparative and applied research on the subject, the collection of testimonies of prominent East Africans involved in processes of constitutional evolution and development, and the promotion of the reform of school and university curricula. EACODEV would also participate in a coordinative effort to bring all those institutions with a regional focus through the exchange of information and the hosting of collaborative initiatives.

2.2 The Process of Regional Consultation

This proposal emerges from a process of intellectual debate and discussion that is as important, in terms of its evolution, as its eventual outcome. The

Working Group on Constitutional Development sought to generate a discussion about a variety of issues relating to leadership, governance and constitutionalism in the East African region. Pursuant to this objective a grant was provided by the Ford Foundation to the Centre for Basic Research (CBR) in order to examine the feasibility of establishing a regional body that deals with constitutional development. To this end, CBR commissioned studies in each of the countries of East Africa to examine the issue through canvassing the opinion of a variety of actors on the scene. At the mid-July 1996 conference on the New Africa Initiative held at Entebbe, Uganda, the Working Group met for the first time and considered developments in the project to date. At the conference, CBR presented a concept paper on the idea of a regional centre for constitutional development. The concept paper was concerned not simply with the notion of such an initiative, but more importantly with its efficacy and implication for the concept of constitutionalism, the idea of regional cooperation and the possibilities of enhanced collaboration with existing initiatives in the region. The CBR study received widespread approval and endorsement from participants at the Initiative conference. Following the Entebbe workshop, the Working Group met in a session in Kampala from 12 - 13 October 1996 and brainstormed on the following dimensions of the project:

1. The mission, vision and objectives of the proposed centre;
2. The structure and scope of the proposed centre;
3. Linkages and collaboration with other actors in the area;
4. Resource and financial mobilization; and
5. The way forward.

The Working Group structured the discussion around the following broad areas/issues, viz.: collaboration and linkages; structure and scope; resource mobilization and finally, the Mission, Vision and Objectives of the initiative. Under the rubric of an organization of the type envisaged, a number of functions which immediately struck the Working Group as feasible. In summary, these included research (basic, applied and comparative); Constitutional activism; Lobbying (as a Constitutional "watch-dog" for the region); Policy formulation and advice; technical assistance within the region and beyond; constitutional reform and revision; debate and discussion, and a whole series of activities rotating around the collection and distribution of information.

Following a discussion on the above matters, the brain-storming session concluded that it was essential to proceed to the actualization of the establishment of EACODEV with a maximum dispatch.

3. Mission, Vision and Objectives

3.1 Broad Mission

The mission of EACODEV is to promote a multi and interdisciplinary dialogue on constitution-making, constitutionalism and democratic governance in the East African Region. It intends to pursue this mission through research, information dissemination, public debate and advocacy.

3.2 Specific Objectives

The specific objectives of EACODEV are the following:

1. To advance the science, processes and art of constitution-making, constitutionalism and democratic governance through basic, comparative and applied research;
2. To commission state-of-the-art studies on various dimensions of constitution-making, constitutionalism and democratic governance in the region;
3. To promote the values and ethos of constitutionalism, and gender equality and equity throughout the East African region;
4. To highlight and address the plight of disadvantaged social, cultural, economic and political groups in the region, including minorities, refugees and people with disabilities;
5. To collect and compile the testimonies of prominent East Africans intricately involved in the processes of constitutional evolution and development in the region, and to foster the contribution of grassroots operatives to these processes;
6. To host an annual lecture by a prominent East African on constitutionalism and constitutional development in East Africa, and to widely disseminate the text of the lecture throughout the region and beyond;
7. To undertake information collection, data banking, archiving, publication and dissemination through the mechanism of seminars, workshops and conferences, and to promote the use of new forms of media and electronic technology in fostering public debate and dialogue;
8. To create and maintain a directory of individuals and institutions committed to the ideals of constitutionalism and democratic governance;

9. To encourage, support and facilitate the reform of school and university curricula incorporating aspects relating to constitution-making, constitutionalism and democratic governance;
10. To act as a regional watchdog for the protection, promotion and enhancement of constitution-making, constitutionalism and democratic governance;
11. To foster solidarity with local, national, regional, and international community groups and organizations; and
12. To offer consultancy and advisory services.

4. Structure, Organization and Process of EACODEV

EACODEV is conceived as an initiative that is to complement rather than supplant those which are already in existence and to address lacunae that have not been targeted. In this respect, it shall be sensitive to and pursue linkages and collaboration with existing initiatives in the same field of operation at the community, national, regional and international levels. Such collaboration would centre around some of the following activities:

a. Training and information exchange, particularly utilizing high-tech facilities such as e-mail and the internet;
b. Exchange of personnel;
c. Co-sponsoring research and publication activities; and
d. Targeting and cooperation with bi-and multilateral institutions (including the international financial institutions, the European Union, the Overseas Development Agency (ODA), Scandinavian funding institutions and organizations (including NOVIB, SIDA and DANIDA). At the regional level, such linkages would target the African Commission on Human and Peoples' Rights, the East African Cooperation and the sub-regional organizations such as COMESA, IGADD, and SADC, among others.

4.1 Structure and Organization

EACODEV shall be:

a. An independent, autonomous, self-sustaining legal entity;

b. Registered as a company limited by guarantee, and headquartered in Kampala (Uganda), with Liaison Offices located in Dar es Salaam (Tanzania), and Nairobi (Kenya);

c. Open to participation (membership) by individuals, statutory corporations and institutions that share in its objectives;

d. Committed to the promotion of regional dialogue and action on the issue of constitutionalism and constitutional development; and

e. Complementary to existing national and regional efforts in the field.

4.2 Organization and Process

EACODEV shall commence operations on an interim basis, with the main Secretariat and liaison offices in each of the three counties functioning as points of contact with individuals and issues therein. During the proposed start-up period of two years, the Secretariat in Uganda shall be established as an independent entity, albeit with close relations with organizations such as Centre for Basic Research(CBR) which have made considerable strides in the arena of constitutional debate and research in Uganda. In Kenya and Tanzania, the Liaison Offices shall in the interim be housed in one of the organizations represented in the Working Group. Such arrangement shall subsist until sufficient resources have been raised to enable EACODEV's Liaisons in the two countries to establish their own independent and self-sustaining operations, which would be linked to the Secretariat in a more decentralized fashion. The process of autonomizing the Liaison Offices will commence alongside the start-up activities of the initiative.

EACODEV shall consist of the following organs:

4.2.1 The Directorate

The EACODEV directorate shall comprise of an executive director (as overall project coordinator), an administrator, a documentalist, an accountant, and a secretary/receptionist. The directorate shall be in charge of the organization of the Centre and the execution of policy objectives as formulated by the Executive Committee. The terms and conditions of the service of members of the Directorate shall be formulated by the Executive Committee.

Liaison Offices in each of the countries of the region shall be responsible to the Executive Director, and shall perform the following functions:

i) establish EACODEV national chapters;
ii) survey and catalogue the various actors operating on the scene;

iii) popularize the objectives of EACODEV in their individual countries; and
iv) organize the execution of the various activities of EACODEV within their specific national contexts.

4.2.2 The Executive Committee

Shall consist of seven (7) members (with a minimum of two drawn from each country in the region and assuring gender parity). The Executive Committee shall act as the governing board of the Centre and formulates general policy through meetings on a quarterly basis, and oversee the promotion and realization of the objectives of EACODEV by the Secretariat. In the interim, the present members of the Working Group on Constitutional Development shall act as the Executive Committee in order to steer the project to a fully operational level. Quorum for the meetings of the Executive Committee shall be 50%, from at least two countries in the region.

4.2.3 The International Advisory Board

The International Advisory Board shall comprise nine (9) imminent East Africans who have distinguished themselves in the arena of constitutionalism, constitutional development and democratic governance. The Board shall meet annually and be charged with:

i. Raising and sustaining an endowment for EACODEV;
ii. Promoting the image of EACODEV within the region and internationally;
iii. Providing intellectual and conceptual support to EACODEV; and
iv. Acting as final arbiter and counsel on issues relating to the operation and performance of EACODEV.

Following the establishment of the Secretariat, the following shall form the short-term elements of the Centre:

a. The creation of a basic research agenda on regional issues;
b. Liaising with all major and minor actors in the field; and
c. Establishing the information clearing house.

5. Resource, Material and Financial Mobilization

The Working Group recognizes that the envisaged project is one that requires substantial resources and support. It considers that resources for EACODEV could emanate from both local and external sources. With respect to the latter, it is most logical to think in terms of a consortium of funders who might be interested in an initiative of this kind, and in particular, of contributing to the creation of an endowment. Such an endowment could cover an initial two year period. In addition, resources would be necessary for the support of the two Liaison Offices in terms of essential equipment and start-up operational funding. To the extent possible, the secretariat and Liaison offices would pursue collaborative initiatives with organizations whose objectives are compatible with those of EACODEV's. This is hoped to reduce overhead expenditures.

With respect to local funding, professional associations (both individual members and collectives); prominent East Africans in the region and abroad, and the business community (local and expatriate) would be approached. EACODEV will also raise moneys through undertaking consultancies on issues of constitutionalism and constitutional development, the payment of membership and subscription fees, and the sale of its publications.

6. Plan of Action

6.1 Short-term Plans

The short-term plans of EACODEV are to establish an interim Secretariat and Liaison Offices in each of the countries of the region, with the brief to:-

i) Float a company limited by guarantee;

ii) Establish national chapters in each of the countries of the region;

iii) Consult with, review and inventory all the actors in the arena of constitutional development and constitutionalism, and explore collaborative and collective methods of approaching the issue on a regional basis;

iv) Commission state-of-the-art studies, and literature and conceptual reviews on the subject;

v) Create a process for the conduct of basic research on pertinent issues of relevance in the region, and in particular, the reconstruction of the constitutional past (precolonial, colonial and post-colonial);

vi) Establish an information-clearing house which would act as the East African port of first call for the pursuit, collection and dissemination of information relating to constitutional issues;

vii) Open and operate an Internet Web-site of constitutional materials from East Africa, including basic laws, judicial decisions, pertinent articles, and regional treaties; and

viii) Organize and host an annual conference of scholars, activists and policy-makers to discuss pertinent issues relating to constitutionalism, constitutional development and democratic process in the region.

The process of registration and establishment (items i to iii above) are to be pursued by the Chairperson and Secretary of the Working Group (Mrs. Solome Bbossa and J. Oloka-Onyango respectively), while all issues relating to the establishment of the Liaison Offices are to be handled by Rose Migiro (Tanzania) and Willy Mutunga (Kenya). Items iv to viii are to be pursued by the established Secretariat with the advice of the members of the Working Group.

6.2 Medium and Long-term Plans

i) Liaise with and establish a working rapport with the Secretariat of the East African Cooperation (EAC). In particular, EACODEV shall act as a think-tank to buttress and strengthen the conceptual and policy operations of the EAC.

ii) With particular respect to issues of relevance to the operation of the EAC, EACODEV shall focus on the following:

   a. The promotion of overall constitutional reform and development at national level and regionally;

   b. Migration, refugees, and free movement in the region;

   c. The control and use of shared resources;

   d. The legal protection of human and peoples' rights and the environment; and

   e. Support for regional judicial activity relating to matters of a constitutional nature.

iii) Carry out comparative and applied policy research;

iv) Create linkages with regional organizations (in Africa and beyond) and think-tanks with similar objectives;

v) Publish comprehensive studies (in book form) of basic, applied and comparative research undertaken by EACODEV;

vi) Departmentalize and strengthen research and advocacy elements of EACODEV. Future departments of EACODEV shall be three in number, viz.:

   a. Constitutional and Comparative Studies;

b. Legal and Constitutional Reform; and
c. Publications, Outreach and Conferences.

PROGRESS REPORT on EACODEV'S ACTIVITIES

(*Presented at the October 1998 Workshop, Nairobi, Kenya*)

The Secretariat was opened in March, 1998 in Kampala, Uganda, and the two liaison offices will soon be opened in Nairobi and Dar es Salaam respectively. Dr. Willy Mutunga and Dr. Rose Migiro are working as liaison officers in Nairobi and Dar es Salaam respectively. In the last six months during which EACODEV has been in place, a number of stakeholders have been identified in Uganda and Kenya and a similar exercise is to be carried out in Tanzania.

Three launch-workshops have been planned with the aim of introducing the organization to various stakeholders and identifying urgent constitutional issues to be addressed in each country. They were also intended to give a direction to the centre based on responses from the region. The first workshop was successfully held in Entebbe Uganda in August 1998. Its main theme was "**Constitutional Reform in East Africa**". Several recommendations emerged from the deliberations by the participants, especially with regard to the draft treaty for the establishment of the East African Community.

The second workshop is scheduled to take place at the beginning of November, 1998 in Mombassa, Kenya. The issues for discussion will be decided upon by our partners in Kenya. The third workshop will take place in Tanzania in December 1998,

EACODEV intends to continue generating debate even after the three launch workshops in the region on issues of leadership, governance and constitutionalizm. Particular emphasis will be placed on political equality, gender issues, the question of refugees and migration, regional integration and other topical matters concerning the peoples of the region. EACODEV has also embarked on the collection and analysis of materials on Constitutionalizm in East Africa. These materials, after collection and compilation in a database, can be utilised by partner organizations. Eventually, EACODEV will have a web page on which it will post a variety of materials of general interest in this area.

FUTURE DIRECTIONS

1. Constitutional Development

With particular respect to issues of relevance to the operation of the East African Community, EACODEV shall focus on the following:

a) The promotion of overall constitutional reform and development at the national level and regionally;

b) Migration, refugees and free movement in the region;

c) The control and use of shared resources;

d) The legal protection of human and peoples' rights and the environment;

e) Support for regional judicial activity relating to matters of a constitutional nature;

f) Comparative and applied policy research;

g) Creating linkages with regional organizations (in Africa and beyond) and think- tanks with similar objectives;

h) Publish comprehensive studies (in book form) of basic, applied and comparative research undertaken by EACODEV;

i) Departmentalize and strengthen research and advocacy elements of EACODEV.

2. Training

EACODEV will link up with the African Commission on Human and peoples' Rights and is in the process of designing a programme for the training of stakeholders within the region on the contents of the protocol for the establishment of the African Court of Human Rights.

Synergy Strategies

- Research within the region, to utilize partner organizations for information collection and research;
- Provide a forum of these key partners to contribute to the debate on constitutionalizm;
- Contribute to the curriculum of the Uongozi School;
- Provide training skills for stakeholders in the fields of democracy and governance; and

- Create a web-page on the Internet on activities of EACODEV.

The stakeholders in the region can also link up through the exchange of ideas in form of a journal which would go a long way in consolidation of the initiative.

Collaborative Measures

The Centre plans to establish an information clearing house which would act as the East African port of first call for the pursuit, collection and dissemination of information related to constitutional issues.

Funding Strategies

We have approached several donors for fundraising which included HIVOS, USAID, and the Ford Foundation.

Other means of raising money suggested include subscription for the Centre to avoid external political intervention and other influences. It is proposed that EACODEV will be all inclusive, and avoid stalemates and squabbles.

Discussion and Exchange of Views (ECOADEV)

Following the presentation on the proposal for the establishment of the Kituo Cha Katiba (ECOADEV), the participants of the workshops made a thorough discussion and exchange of views pertaining to a wide range of issues. These included funding/financing the programmes, strategies to be adopted, opportunities and challenges to be encountered in due course, and expected outcomes from the undertaking. Moreover, several key questions were raised during the session, and pertinent responses were given by those concerned.

On the subject of soliciting financial support for the project, identifying and approaching potential sources of funding was considered as the immediate task. It was also stated that caution should be made so that donors may not influence the project by attaching strings that could undermine its objectives. Mention was also made about seeking ways and means for reducing the extent of perpetual dependence on donors so that activities could be carried out without interruption and on a sustainable basis. In this regard, it was noted that there is a need for mulilateralizing sources of support in the form of instituting a consortium of donors.

A number of strategies presumed to facilitate endeavours were suggested by the participants in the course of the discussion and exchange of views. These included the need for assisting policy makers and groups struggling for the entrenchment of democratic values and practice in the region and conducting periodic/annual consultation sessions. This could be done by bringing in well-informed East Africans together, compiling the biographies of prominent East Africans involved in the struggle for democracy, instituting an information clearing house at the centre, making preparations to operate as a watchdog to criticize and lobby on matters of constitutional concern, working towards promoting solidarity among like-minded groups at the regional and international levels, and laying the basis for reforming school and university curricula.

In the list of possible opportunities and challenges, the following were raised:

Opportunities

a) Given the new developments and recently introduced changes in the international system, ECOADEV can take a clear ideological position in the context of the "New World Order";

b) The existence of discredited political systems and leaderships will likely lead to the creation of a formidable constituency of support in favor of change.

Challenges/Constraints

a) There is a need to clearly demarcate the focus of activities, between research and activism, as the major undertaking of the Centre;

b) The Centre should prioritize activities, and avoid duplicating what other organizations are already doing;

c) Issues pertinent to each country should be specifically discerned and be dealt with accordingly;

d) The Centre should reach the rural people and address such issues associated with land, poverty, and ethnicity that are relevant to their everyday life;

e) There is a danger that in some cases the acquisition of funds could entail political conditionalities from providers; and

f) Problems could be faced in finding a knowledgeable/experienced and committed leadership to run the Secretariat.

Participants also envisaged that instituting ECOADEV could result in bringing about the unity of East African activists and academics on the issues of democracy and constitutionalism. It was also hoped that if this is realized, there would be a chance for effectively challenging the *status quo*. The full-fledged launching of the Centre was also viewed as a factor that could immensely contribute towards developing strategies that are congruent with the African reality thereby avoiding irrelevant and gross prescriptions by foreigners.

4

EAST AFRICAN UONGOZI INSTITUTE

Rwekaza Mukandala[•]

1. Introduction

The East African region, like the rest of Africa, has been facing many challenges since the mid-1980s which require a qualitatively different breed of leaders than those who were groomed under the one-party systems and military regimes. The challenge that concerns us here is that of coping with, and shaping and managing the many changes that are taking place locally, regionally and globally. These require leaders who are imaginative, innovative and cosmopolitan in outlook.

The problem is seen as the absence of dynamism, initiative and vision among leaders. Three causes account for the problem. First, the monolithic one-party and military, (in the case of Uganda) heritage fostered authoritarian and uncompetitive elite. Second, the countries concerned have generally accorded low priority to leadership training, especially during the current period of economic hardships. Third, the civil society in East Africa is still relatively weak due to post-independence destruction of autonomous institutions, and therefore cannot challenge (awaken) the ruling elite effectively or call it into accountability. The effects have been resource cutbacks for institutions of higher learning, reduction of training programmes and the poorly trained, local generation of leaders. Thus the need to change this situation is clear and urgent.

2. Objectives of the East African Uongozi Institute

The overall objective of the Institute is the creation of a dynamic and broad-minded leadership in the East African region. This should be referred to as the

[•] Director, East African Uongozi Institute, Dar es Salaam, Tanzania.

"Development Objective". To achieve this objective, a number of "intermediate" (or supportive) objectives must be achieved.

1. Providing leadership training to over 200 carefully selected students leadership training at the Uongozi School through well-planned annual training programmes;
2. Increasing knowledge of leadership-related problems and issues in East Africa and elsewhere through research, publications and documentation;
3. Establishing functional links with key stakeholders (NGOs and public institutions) in the East African region by creating a solid network of information dissemination;
4. Providing advisory and mid-career follow-up training to EAUI graduates and other interested public servants in East Africa through appropriate programs; and
5. Developing a global critical constituency support.

3. Implementation Strategies

The implementation of the East African Uongozi Institute's mission has, so far, been carried out through three strategies, viz: the Uongozi School training programme, Networking and co-ordinated activities by the University of California at Los Angeles (UCLA).

3.1 Uongozi School

The **Uongozi School** hopes to provide a forum for exchange of ideas and research experience among top-notch students from East Africa, and elsewhere; and experienced scholars, policy makers, and individuals in leadership positions in East Africa and elsewhere.

3.1.1 Recruitment process

The recruitment of the Uongozi School participants went through a two stage process. First, a provisional list of 15 students was made from the list of applicants at each centre. Second, a final selection of participants was made from the lists of provisionally selected participants to attain the allotted quota at each centre- 10 participants from each of the Universities of Dar es Salaam, Makerere, and Nairobi, and 9 participants from the University of California, Los Angeles (2 Graduate students were also added to the team).

In addition, there was one self-sponsored participant from Denmark in the 1998 Uongozi School training program.

To execute the two stages of the recruitment process committees were formed at all the four centres - Makerere University, University of Nairobi, University of Dar es Salaam, and University of California, Los Angeles.

3.1.2 Composition of the participants

3.1.2.1 Gender

One of the points raised in the project proposal is the gender dimension. It is explicitly stated in the proposal that not less than one third of the participants will be females.

It is gratifying to note that of the 42 participants of the 1998 Uongozi School, 24 (57 per cent) were females and 18 (43 per cent) were males. The gender composition from each of the four centres, however, varied. Table 1 below presents the gender composition of the participants by centre of origin.

Table 1: Gender Composition of the 1998 Uongozi School Participants by Center

Centre	Numbers			Percentages		
	Females	Males	Total	Female	Males	Total
University of Dar es Salaam	4	6	10	40	60	100
University of Nairobi	6	4	10	60	40	100
Makerere University	4	6	10	40	60	100
American Universities	10	1	11	91	9	100
University of Copenhagen	0	1	1	0	100	100
Total	24	18	42	57	43	100

3.1.2.2 Disciplines

Another aspect on participants raised in the project proposal is the composition of academic disciplines. In the project proposal, it is stated that students of the Uongozi School will be drawn from the disciplines of Political Science, Public Policy and Administration, Sociology, History, Economics, Business Administration, Commerce, Law, Education, the natural Sciences and other related fields.

Table 2: Discipline Composition of the 1998 Uongozi School Participants

Discipline	Number
Political Science and Public Administration	9
Government	3
Law	3
Political Science and Sociology	1
Social Sciences	1
Business Administration	1
Politics	1
History of East Africa	1
Mechanical Engineering	1
Literature and History	1
Political Science and Economics	1
Economics and Sociology	1
International Studies	1
Social Administration and Economics	1
Economics	2
Anthropology	1
Accounting	1
Sociology, Afro-American, African Studies	1
Commerce	1
Political Science and Social Administration	1
Economics, Geography, and Sociology	1
Land Use Planning, Environmental Studies	1
Social Administration and Literature	1
Economics and Mathematics	1
Sociology	1
Political Science and Anthropology	1
History of Science (History of disease)	1
African, American Studies and International Development Studies	
Social Welfare and Administration	1
Total	**42**

Although the Political Science discipline seems to have had the largest representation as shown in Table 2 above, the spirit of the project proposal has been widely satisfied because as many as 27 different disciplines were represented.

3.1.2.3 Universities

The participants of the Uongozi School came from as many as 12 Universities (3 Universities in East Africa, 8 Universities in the United States, and 1 University in Europe). The distribution of participants from various institutions in the 1998 Uongozi School programs is given in Table 3 below.

Table 3: Participants of the 1998 Uongozi School by University

University	Number of Participants
University of Dar es Salaam	10
University of Nairobi	10
Makerere University	10
University of California, Los Angeles	4
Monmouth University	1
Stanford University	1
MaCalaster College	1
Indiana University	1
Reed College	1
Wellesley College	1
Harvard University	1
University of Copenhagen	1
Total	**42**

3.1.3 Programme

The Uongozi School programme combined formal studies with educational visits to interesting historical sites.

3.1.3.1 Formal studies

The formal studies theme for the 1998 Uongozi School was **GOVERNANCE, DEMOCRACY, AND DEVELOPMENT.** The theme was considered under 5 modules, namely:

MODULE 1: Theoretical, Methodological, and Historical Perspectives
MODULE 2: State Formation and Political Transitions

MODULE 3: Development, Structural Adjustment Reforms and Resource Dynamics
MODULE 4: Civil Society, Empowerment, Democracy and Governance
MODULE 5: Informatics, Culture and Communication

Modules 2 and 4 were co-ordinated by members of the organizing committee whereas Modules 1, 3, and 5 were co-ordinated by resource persons who are not members of the organizing committee. The Module Co-ordinators and Sub-themes of the Modules were as detailed below.

MODULE 1 - Co-ordinator: Professor Issa Shivji
Sub-themes

- Society, economics and politics in East Africa.
- The historical experience of integration efforts in East Africa: from pre-colonial to the present times.
- Nationalism, regionalism, and pan-Africanism: The ideas of connectedness and networking.
- East Africa in Africa and the global order.

MODULE 2 - Co-ordinator: Professor Akiiki B Mujaju

Sub-themes
- State formation in East Africa.
- Political structures and institutions in East Africa.
- Political transition from one party system to other political systems.
- Ethnicity, politics and ethnic conflicts.
- Constitution and the rule of law.
- The evolution of the concept and practice of Human Rights.

MODULE 3 - Co-ordinator: Professor Severine Rugumamu

Sub-themes
- Economic development and resource management.
- Employment, entrepreneurship and the informal sector.
- Gender and development policies.
- Transparency, accountability and ethics in public policy.
- Technology policy and scientific progress.
- Socio-political context of structural adjustment programs, including development aid and trade liberalization.
- Population, environment and development.
- Sustainable development in the African context.

MODULE 4- Co-ordinator: Professor Edmond Keller

Sub-themes

- The idea and formation of the civil society in East Africa.
- Democracy and democratization.
- Gender issues in democracy.
- On power distribution and empowerment.
- The concept of Governance and its applications in East Africa
- Governance, leadership, and leadership style/qualities.

MODULE 5- Co-ordinator: Professor Penina Mlama

Sub-themes

- Communication, culture and development.
- Performing Arts, popular theatre and development.
- Mass media, mediation and image creation.
- Freedom of the press and responsible journalism.
- Public relations and speech-making.
- Communication skills.

The formal studies approach was by lecture presentations followed by open discussions. In addition to the open discussions, participants had an opportunity to pursue points in seminar group discussions. The participants were divided into two discussion groups of 20, each led by a graduate student. In the discussion groups, participants were expected to analyse and discuss the points raised in the lectures or picked in the readings. In this way, the participants could help each other to better follow the program and benefit more from it. The discussion groups were scheduled to meet twice a week. Furthermore, in three cases a panel discussion approach was adopted in lieu of the normal lectures. At the end of each Module, an assignment was given to the participants to assess the knowledge gained from the presentations and the required readings.

3.1.3.2 Study visits

Participants visited sites of historical and cultural significance in Bagamoyo, Zanzibar, and Arusha, all in Tanzania, and in Jinja and Kampala, both in Uganda. While in Bagamoyo, the participants first visited the Kaole ruins, and later they were shown the place were slaves were kept before being transported to their final destinations. Lastly, the participants visited the Catholic Church Museum.

The first destination in Zanzibar was the Maruhubi Palace ruins, one of the famous places constituting the ancient monuments of Zanzibar. From the Maruhubi Palace ruins the participants visited the spice farms where they saw, tasted, and bought various spices of the Zanzibar Island. This was a memorable and learning experience to all the participants. Subsequently, the participants visited the Jozani forest to see the red calboush monkeys and finally stopped at the old slave town, and in particular the Lutheran Cathedral to see the tunnel in which slaves were dumped before they were transported to their final destinations. Many traces of the cruelty done to the slaves, including the chains used to tie them together, are visible in the tunnel.

In Kampala, the participants first visited the Namugongo Roman Catholic Church built in commemoration of the 22 Ugandan Christian martyrs who were ordered to be killed by Kabaka Mwanga for following a foreign religion and refusing to give it up. At the same sight, the participants were shown the exact spot where the killings took place. In Jinja the participants visited the source of the White Nile, and some used this rare opportunity to ride in canoes up to the actual place which marks the source of the river. Next, the participants visited the Bujagali falls. The visits continued with a guided tour of the Uganda National Museum where the participants saw lots of things associated with the past Ugandan way of life. with a historical perspective. From the Uganda National Museum, the participants proceeded to the Kasubi tombs, where the kings of Buganda are buried.

While in Uganda, Dr Abel Rwendeire, the Minister of State for Higher education addressed the participants. It was originally expected that the participants would have an audience with the Prime Minister of Uganda, Mrs. Specioza. This did not materialize owing to her illness.

During the Arusha tour, the participants first made a brief stop at the Cultural Heritage where there was plenty to see concerning the culture of a number of ethnic groups in Tanzania. From there, the participants went to Lake Manyara Game Park where they saw different animals and birds, and also toured the Ngorongoro crater where they saw herds of animals of different types.

3.1.4 Resource persons

The Uongozi School benefited from the services of 32 resource persons. Of these, 8 were females and 24 were males. There were resource persons from Kenya, Uganda, Nigeria, Zimbabwe, England, Denmark, the United States, and Tanzania.

3.2 Networking

- In November 1997, the Director of the Institute attended a panel discussion on the East African Uongozi Institute at the African Studies Association(ASA) conference, in Columbus, Ohio. This was a good opportunity where the Institute was introduced to the North American and other scholars.

- The East African Uongozi Institute has already established contacts with the East Africa Co-operation Secretariat by getting the Executive Secretary of the secretariat to launch the Institute and the Uongozi School. In his opening speech, the Executive Secretary emphasised the need for future co-operation between the Secretariat and the East African Uongozi Institute.
- There is a good working relationship between the Institute and the African Association of Political Science (AAPS). The Association sponsored two resource persons for the 1998 Uongozi School training program.
- The East African Uongozi Institute informed all the associated members of the New Africa initiative about the Institute's programmes. In actual fact one person associated with the New Africa Initiative gave a speech to the 1998 Uongozi School participants.
- There is a good working relationship between the press in Tanzania and the East African Uongozi Institute. At its launching, the Institute received a wide press coverage.
- The Institute has also been introduced to a number of Non-Governmental organizations.
- Most importantly, the East African Uongozi Institute had developed a good rapport with the Administrations and colleagues at the four Universities. More significantly, of the four Universities have pledged to remain committed to support the objectives of the Institute.
- Brochures and posters were produced in order to popularize the aims and objectives of the Institute.

4. Future Directions

4.1 Strategic Plan

The East African Uongozi Institute has prepared a Strategic Plan covering the period 1997- 2001. The Institute has four related components, namely,

- The Uongozi School(UOS);
- Research, Publication and Documentation(RPD);
- Networking and Information Dissemination(NID); and
- Advisory and Follow-up Training Services(AFTS).

4.2 Components of the East African Uongozi Institute

The components of the EAUI have the following intermediate objectives peculiar to each of them:

1. Component A: The Uongozi School (UOS)

This component will handle all activities relating to the organization and conducting of the annual leadership training programmes. It will be known as the **Uongozi School** of EAUI.

2. Component B: Research, Publications and Documentation (RPD)

The RPD will be responsible for organizing and conducting research, ensuring publication of research findings, and proper documentation and distribution of relevant literature to facilitate the annual training programmes. Emphasis will be on two types of research, namely leadership-related research and research on the "burning issues" of the day which include issues related to East African co-operation, as will be defined by the Project Steering Committee.

3. .Component C: Networking, and Information Dissemination(NID)

This will be responsible for creating an "East African constituency," of people concerned with the leadership factor. These actors, to be considered as the "stakeholders" of EAUI, will be identified from such different sectors as the East African Co-operation Secretariat, government agencies, the business, academic, and voluntary/NGO sectors. This component will attempt to link these stakeholders through various ways, including seminars, workshops, conferences, and distribution of EAUI newsletters and bulletins.

4. Component D: Advisory and Follow-up Training Services (AFTS)

AFTS will be responsible for organizing and conducting follow-up training courses for mid-career public servants and leaders who will include former EAUI graduates and other interested persons. The component will also respond to specific requests from any of the major stakeholders, e.g. learning institutions, the civil service, the East African Co-operation, voluntary sector groups, etc. The requests from stakeholders may take different forms, e.g. advice on a specific issue, mounting a specialized leadership training courses for particular groups, conducting research on a specified issues, etc. It is believed that AFTS has the potential for becoming a source of funding for EAUI through the sale of professional services.

With regard to the activities of the Uongozi School, the following recommendations were made:

1. Background information on East Africa be sent to the selected Uongozi School participants who are not from East Africa, as soon as they are identified.
2. Norms and code of conduct governing the operation of the Uongozi School be established.
3. Enough time should be allocated during the orientation period to discuss the norms and guidelines on formal lectures and study visits.
4. Arrangements be made for the Uongozi School participants to interact with a nearby community (for example youth organizations) at some stage in the programme.
5. Practical sessions where participants can actually practice some aspects of what they cover in the formal lectures be increased.
6. The administrative team be reinforced to include an academic supervisor to deal with the academic matters of the Uongozi School.
7. Arrangements for the 1999 Uongozi School should start immediately.
8. Internships should be organized in 1999 for the 1998 Uongozi School participants.

5. Assumptions, Risks and Sustainability

The East African Uongozi Institute project rests on the following four assumptions:

1. That the four co-operating universities which "own" the project will sustain the current interest and enthusiasm through the period 1997-2001 and beyond.
2. That the project will ENLIST stakeholders and clients who will make use of its services.
3. That the governments and other actors in the region will continue to sustain the democratization trajectory which has been set in motion and which is essential for grooming the kind of leadership envisaged by the project.

4. That the relatively stable political and economic situation currently prevalent in the region will survive the destabilizing currents coming from the surrounding areas.

The third and the fourth assumptions stated above also spell out three potential risks which may face the project. These are:

1. Democratic changes in the region may be slow (and reversals cannot be discounted in fragile political conditions), in which case the existing authoritarian elements in the region may continue to smoother the emergency of a truly dynamic and democratic leadership.
2. The political turmoil in the central African region may spill-over to the East African region and render institutionalised leadership training difficult.
3. The fragile economies in East Africa may continue to face slow growth (or even deteriorate),leading to further cuts in resources going to educational institutions. Such a scenario would make the project totally dependent on external resources.

The purpose of spelling out assumptions and risks is to "sensitize" those involved so that they are constantly aware of the huddles which the project may face. Indeed, effective management of the risks itself is an important aspect of the leadership training programme of the EAUI project.

As mentioned above, one potential risk is that the project might continue to depend on external resources beyond the period 1997 - 2001. It is therefore important that ways of making the project financially self-supporting are conceived at the beginning. The following sources and strategies are envisaged in this regard:

1. The Ford Foundation is envisaged to be the initial core donor. Other donors should also be approached to contribute.*
2. This may be a small source at the beginning due to the current economic problems facing the East African region but is expected to grow as their economies improve.**

---

*Mobilization of financial support from donors who support the objectives of EAUI.

** Mobilization for funding, from national government budgets, through the auspices of the co-operating universities.

3. This source constitutes the stakeholders of EAUI along with the four universities which own the project.***
4. Growth of this source is dependent on the popularity of the EAUI training programmes.****
5. **Sale of EAUI publications; Fees from advisory and training services tailored for mid-career leaders and public servants** (in accordance with the mandate given to the Advisory and Follow-up Training Services Component of the project).

6. Synergy Strategies

The East African Uongozi Institute cherishes the idea of working out a synergy. Co-operation may be achieved as follows:

1. Partners to be invited to participate in activities of the Uongozi School.
2. Research findings and publications of partners should be used by EAUI.
3. Partners should be requested to provide some of their products or services to the EAUI.
4. Partners can take on some of the interns to enable them reinforce the knowledge and training gained at the Uongozi School.

THE CO-OPERATION BETWEEN THE EAUI AND UCLA

Edmond J. Keller

The New African Initiative (NAI) was seen in the context of emerging publications and efforts of African scholars who have demonstrated commitment in articulating the African voice - a voice that is engaging the process of globalization. Just to name a few examples: the works of Tandika Mukandawire when he was with CODESRIA, and Jonathan Moyo's multi-media project, "*The Making of New Africa*". Africans want to engage the

*** Mobilization of support from private and voluntary organizations in East Africa which share the objectives of EAUI.

**** **Collection of fees** from foreign and (some) local students who participate in the programme.

process of globalization rather than ignoring it, or running away from it. That is what the New Africa initiative is all about and coincides with the Ford Foundation's efforts in the past two years.

In the United States, the Ford Foundation has been funding university projects that address cross-border and cross-cultural concerns and build bridges to fill gaps among the various disciplines. That seems to be how UCLA came into this particular picture. UCLA was already doing some collaborative work with the Universities of Dar es Selam and Nairobi which helped it to be familiar with such initiatives.

UCLA has a couple of grants from the Ford Foundation. One of them is to work with this synergy workshop to help develop and disseminate information about the "New Africa Initiative" in the United States. In this area, we have worked with Dr. Teka on the first synergy workshop. We also hosted around table where a number of participants were represented at the last African Studies Association Conference. We had presentations from Dr. Mukandla, Dr. Somjee, myself, Assumta Oturu all of whom informed their American audience about what was going on with the NAI.

UCLA became involved in the synergy workshop on the Uongozi Institute earlier. We were invited by the Program Officer of the Ford Foundation to think about situating UCLA as part of the NAI. During the early stages of the initiation of the Uongozi School, UCLA provided education materials, and other kinds of educational resources, computer hardware and software and books. It also undertook the production of recruitment materials, and involved in the recruitment of students from the United States who were encouraged to have first hand experience by living in Africa and interacting with Africans. UCLA hopes that by making such interactions, misconceptions and stereotypes could be overcome. The Uongozi Institute serves the purpose of breaking down those barriers. UCLA also agreed to identify placement opportunities for Uongozi fellows once they complete their training at the EAUI. In this regard, places where some students can be put were identified in the United States or in Africa.

UCLA has a multi-year national summit on Africa, which is broken down into regional summits. Two of such gatherings have been held so far and there remain an additional six to be convened in the coming few years. UCLA is funded by the Ford Foundation to organize public education forums which are used to familiarize the African voice to the American context. The whole idea of doing this is to build a constituency for Africa.

U.S. policy towards Africa has three components:

1) Democracy and human rights
2) Trade and investment
3) Peace and security

Bearing in mind the fact that trade and investment can not be promoted in the absence of the other two, our public forums concentrate on the mutuality of the three areas. The idea of underscoring the three components of U.S. policy is to get American citizens who are not aquatinted with the African reality got informed. It is believed that if they are informed, they will try to positively influence U.S. policy on Africa.

UCLA's involvement with the three African Universities and all those participating in the NAI is a milestone in international collaboration. This is in line with what the Ford Foundation wanted to accomplish when undertakings in this regard were initiated few years back. The achievements registered until now have proved that the goals stated are realizable.

Discussion and Exchange of Views (EAUI)

The participants raised a number of points during the session that accompanied the presentation on the East African Uongozi Institute (EAUI). These included the adopted strategies for running activities, the anticipated opportunities accruing from the program components, and the results expected from the venture.

With regard to the program aspects, it was envisaged that the strategies designed to facilitate undertakings will focus on lectures, debates, and training on scientific inquiry and interactive learning. The programs are also expected to incorporate internship exercises based on field visits that are aimed at providing students with a practical understanding and appreciation of the underlying objectives of the Institute.

It was hoped that the launching of the project could avail opportunities in terms of supplementing existing university curriculum, promoting practical (out-of-class) training, offering a forum for trainees through which they can interact with policy makers, civic leaders and prominent intellectuals.

The participants expressed their belief that the programs of EAUI could result in grooming a new brand of imaginative and dynamic leaders, and generate research outputs that could serve as a basis for policy debates.

During the discussion session, participants appreciated the support provided and the pledges made to facilitate endeavors on the part of the Vice Chancellors of the co-operating Universities and the Chief Executive of the East African Secretariat. One participant suggested that the curriculum of the EAUI should give more room for interactions among students and means and ways of inviting young leaders to brief trainees on difficulties to be encountered when disposing leadership functions. It was also proposed that training components must include developing skills that could help in using modern information technology and the crafts of multi-media (films, novels, plays...).

Questions on a variety of concerns like the compatibility of EAUI training sessions with a typical university system, plans for including trainees outside universities, and possibilities for including students from other African countries outside East Africa were raised. Explanation on why a large number (25%) of students from the United States were enrolled in the EAUI training programs. Resource persons and the concerned individuals responded to the queries in a satisfactory manner.

5

SERIES ON ALTERNATIVE RESEARCH IN EAST AFRICA TRUST: *Rebuilding Local Knowledge Industry in East Africa*

Mutahi G. Ngunyi

1. Introduction

The New Africa Initiative is about Transition in East Africa. It is about, *inter alia,* the 'new politics' of the region. The *raison d'être* of SAREAT, as a component of this Initiative, is therefore derived from the position that East Africa is currently experiencing a new political dispensation. The process of this transition has generated much interest for methodological, empirical and theoretical investigations. But in spite of this flora of 'new knowledge', an *East African position* regarding the 'new politics' of the region is yet to buoy.

SAREAT therefore argues for the provision of a forum through which East African development and rights activists, scholars, and the democratic challengers can develop and broadcast an indigenous position regarding the 'new politics' of the region.[1] The idea here is to put to debate existing policy, methodological and theoretical positions regarding the region with emerging empirical findings generated by East Africans. In this way, we hope to set in motion the process of rebuilding the local knowledge industry in East Africa and to provide the East African with the opportunity to take the initiative for setting the policy and research agenda for the region. And it is in this context that SAREAT hopes to present some *East African Alternatives* to policy, theory, and methodology in the area of democratic politics, constitutional reforms, social policy and transformation, economic conditionality and development provisioning.

The idea of *East African Alternatives* derives from the argument that the policies of transition in East Africa have failed to take into account certain

[1] Why is this important anyway? We shall answer this question in a while.

conditions prevailing on the 'policy sites'.[2]This is largely because the policy and agenda makers in the reform process are for the most part informed by 'research tourists' who visit the 'site' for few weeks and make overwhelming policy recommendations which are in turn translated into sweeping interventions. While these interventions have worked in the short-run, in the long run, their inability to capture certain social and political actors in civil society formations, have a local interpretation to the on-going reform process in the region- but an interpretation that has been muted through historical conditioning. SAREAT therefore hopes to give voice to these actors and to provide for the missing link in the formulation of the reform agenda by both the local and international actors.

2. The New East Africa

If the New Africa Initiative is about Transition and 'new politics' in the region, what are the elements of this transition and what is 'new' about them. Generally, there has been the de-militarisation of politics in Uganda, the re-invention of regime types in Kenya and Tanzania and the rise of a fairly bonafide oppositionist force in all the three. Apart from the above, four elements of transition in East Africa (among others) are worth mentioning.

2.1 Constitutional Reforms

One enduring political development in East Africa in the 1990s has to do with the contractual relationship between the independence state and the general citizenry. The grounds on which this contract was negotiated have since become obsolete and calls for its re-negotiation dominate politics in East Africa today. In both Kenya and Tanzania, the process of constitution-making, as a process of re-negotiating the contract binding the individual to the state, is in progress. This process has already been completed in Uganda, although post-constitution accommodations are still being put in place. The achievements made so far notwithstanding, the challenges of constitution-making are bound to dominate the politics of the region for decades to come.

The enduring policy and 'research question' in this area will be whether the constitution is a viable means through which the individual can exert influence on the government, and at the same time pursue and protect his/her interest through its instruments. Undoubtedly, this raises the issue of popular participation in the whole process of constitution-making. A more fundamental research question in the region has to do with the citizen's

---

[2] See for instance Institute of Policy Analysis and Researach (IPAR)'s comments on *The Wolrld Bank Country Framework for Kenya* (Place of publication:? 1996)

general *orientation* towards a constitution. That is, his or *her knowledge* of and *belief in* a constitution as a tool for interest mediation, his *or her feelings* about its role in ensuring political fairplay, and his or *her judgements and opinions* about it as a viable social contract binding all individuals to a commonwealth of al l.[3]

This question of an individual's faith in the constitution as the means through which he or she can moderate his/her relationship is at the center of the impending constitutional crisis in East Africa. More so because what we have in the East African states are two contesting constitutional relationships - one traditional, while the other is republican. Constitution-making discourses in East Africa have only focused on the 'republican' process without examining the forces that undermine it – i.e. the traditional constitutional relationships. This will be a major area of interest for SAREAT - both in its research programme and its publications.

2.2 Civil Society and the Push for Limited Government

During the modernisation debates of the 1960s, discussions on African politics centred on the question of 'degree of government'. Policy advocacy pushed for 'more' government and limited traditional life. Discourse has now gone full cycle advocating for an elaborate associational life and limited government.

The rise of civil society has introduced a 'third force' to the politics of the individual countries in the region. Civil society has become the site for *bona fide* popular agitation for social transformation and political change. In particular, the emergence of a Democracy and Governance (DG) sector of civil society populated by rights activists and people-to-people institutions has galvanised popular democratic claims from 'below'.

In a sense, this has taken part of the political initiative away from the 'political class' which is a significantly new way of 'organising for politics'. Although the DG sector is still in its formative stages in all the three countries, it has great democratic potential and this is probably why policy research (in particular) has focused much of its attention on the sector lately.

The push for a limited government and the rise of a post-developmentalist civil society in East Africa has undoubtedly given rise to a new form of politics and actors in the region. This development has incidentally attracted advocacy, activist and research activities, a mix that has provided an extensive

[3] See Talcott Parsons and Edward Shils, *Toward a General Theory of Action* (Cambridge: 1951). The two refer to this as the cognitive, affective and evaluative orientaitons of the individual.

empirical flora. Indeed, both empirical and theoretical research have been conducted regarding these 'new forms of politics'. The results of these research works have unfortunately not been interrogated or put to debate with each other.

At the level of practice, the DG organisations have articulated their interests using 'global' notions of rights. This is probably because there are no local models of rights activism suitable for their work. Through its publications SAREAT hopes to inform the activities of the DG sector with local and 'appropriate' models of democratic activism. These models shall be derived from on-going research and development work in the rural frontier of civil society or what the DG organisations call 'grassroots'.

2.3 Development as Rights Activism

At independence, it became a practice for the state to 'co-opt' the most vibrant aspects of culture and tradition and apply it to its politics. The ruling elite used it to popularise its development blueprints in the three countries. Indeed, *African Socialism* as embedded in the *Sessional Paper number 10* of 1965 in Kenya, *Ujamaa* under the *Arusha Declaration of 1967* in Tanzania, and the *Common Man's_Charter of 1968* under Obote I, were essentially *traditional apologetics* blended with 'globalised' modes of production.

In this way, traditional values were merged with development strategy and then moralised. This marriage between development, instrumentalised tradition, and state politics saw the birth of indigenous movements like *Harambee*.[4] The mushrooming of local level self-help groups in East Africa can also be seen as a result of this marriage.

The state's early 'capture' of traditional forms of life has apparently insulated this social sphere from agents of democratisation. Civil society actors operate outside of it. The only time they encounter it is when they travel to the grassroots movements to 'empower' them. Yet historically, cultural and traditional resistance movements in East Africa were civil society based.

In Tanzania, *the Maji Maji* and *Hehe* rebellions early in the century were religious resistance movements based in civil society. The *Mau Mau* and Nandi resistance movements in Kenya were cultural rebellions expressed in political terms. Similarly, the *Dini Ya Musambwa,* and *Legio Maria* in Kenya were religious protest movements based in rural civil society. The traditional

[4] This is a fund-raising strategy for internal self-reliance. Although dominant in Kenya, it is also present in Uganda and Tanzania.

religious movements in Uganda in the first half of the 80s were also civil society formations.[5]

The process of liberalisation has not seen such a civil society upsurge. Not only because the traditional forms of expression have been captured by the state, but also because the rural civil society is basically politicised by the democratic challengers from above and not from within itself. To the contrary, the state in East Africa has politicised rural civil society from within, through traditional forms of authority and development provision.

Within the rural civil society itself, however, there is a group of traditional formations which has began a rebellion against state patronage. This inchoate group is more present in Kenya and Tanzania and it attempts to falsify the 1960 nationalist argument that 'democracy should come in small installments behind development'. It casts development in terms of rights and is agitating for the democratisation of the development space arguing that development can not take place in an undemocratic environment. The essence of this activism is therefore to revise this notion and to underscore the fact that development provisioning is a constitutional concern, not a privilege. Especially so after the collapse of the developmentalist state[6].

Certain civil institutions have began linking this thinking with the promotion of second generation rights.[7] Although this development is still new, it has in a sense been captured especially by research work in the area of policy advocacy. The most interesting result from this research has to do with the role of women in development activism. Close to 80% of the organisations situated in the rural frontier of civil society are women groups. Attempts to involve the rural woman in democratisation by the DG sector has however been elusive largely because this has been by way of promotion of first generation rights.

Given the new wave of development activism and the promotion of second generation rights in the rural frontier or civil society, SAREAT hopes to broadcast this alternative method of democratisation as captured by development workers and researchers in East Africa. The role of the woman as an 'anatomistic'[8] individual, that is as an individual who is fairly liberated from partriachial guardianship, will particularly interest our work.

---

[5] For instance, the Alice Lakwena cult.

[6] The developmentalist state derived its *raison d'être* from providing development. The crisis of development in the 1980s has seen development provisioning in East Africa more controlled by the NGOs and less by the state.

[7] Oxfam for instance has numerous position papers on this issue.

[8] Ula Uviolera, *Negotiating a New Gender Contract*, (IDS, Helsinki:1995).

2.4 New Economic Formations

Unlike in the past where three decades of independence where any form of capital had to fraternise with the state in order to survive, economic liberalisation in the 90s has seen the development of 'new economic formations' that are fairly independent of state patronage. This is largely because liberalisation in East Africa has freed the business community from paying 'political taxes' in order to get licenses and government tenders. This in turn has given the business community some political latitude – at least in Kenya and Tanzania. Although these new formations are still inchoate, their development could contribute positively to the transition process in East Africa.The process of democratic transition has not only brought about new forms of politics but new actors as well. The roles of these actors in the process of democratic transition are constantly changing as new challenges emerge with the transition process. Because of their "newness", most of their activities advance independent, sometimes oblivious, of each other. They do not inform, or dialogue with, one another. Sometimes their activities overlap and advance at cross-purposes. This has tended to slow down the process of democratisation in East Africa.

It should however be noted that there is interaction among the new social movements and the new economic formations across the borders of the three East African countries. This interaction accounts in part for the process of *co-operation from below* as opposed to the traditional form of co-operation in East Africa which is driven from *above* by the three heads of state.

Interaction between the different actors within the three countries and across the borders is however limited. And when it happens, it is for a specific practical purpose like the running of a joint project. There is little dialogue over the challenges facing each set of actors and the experiences gained from involvement in the process of transition. As a result, each actor faces their challenges alone without the benefit of the experiences of other actors[9]. Indeed the sharing of these experiences and instituting mechanisms of dialogue would contribute meaningfully to democratic transition in the region.

[9] Some form of dialogue is currently developing in Kenya between policy research organisations, the bureaucracy, social movements and political parties. Several public forums involving these actors have been held to examine such questions as Citizenship and Ethnicity, the Asian Question in East Africa, and the Constitution-Making process in Kenya.

3. The Opportunities

3.1 To capture the politics of a given political moment in East Africa - i.e.: the democratic transition. This is like the transition from colonial rule to independence in the 1960s. The opportunity here is therefore that of documenting, analysing and interpreting this political moment. As the idiom goes "a problem well defined is as good as half solved". Hence, explaining the dynamics of the transition and broadcasting the same will provide impetus to the activities of the democratic challengers.

3.2 To capture the different discourses taking place within the different 'transition sites (eg: civil society, economic sphere etc.) and to have these sites dialogue with each other. This dialogue should be within and between each all the East African countries. Currently, if dialogue exists within each of the countries, little goes beyond the borders to benefit the neighbouring countries. The opportunity for SAREAT then is that of distilling the best methodologies and approaches in development provisioning, rights activism, and democratic advocacy in each of the transition sites and sharing the same with all the other sites in East Africa.

3.3 In the past, policy reform makers have basically been informed by 'research tourists' who visit the 'policy site' for a few weeks and then make generalised positions on the East African economic and political site. In the ultimate end, policy options have been based on an incomplete situation analysis. This is what accounts for the failure of certain reform instruments like 'political conditionality' – at least in Kenya and Uganda. Given this situation, the opportunity for SAREAT is that of incorporating indigenous thought into the process of 'planning for transition'. The involvement of local analysts in this process will not only supplement the position taken by 'reform consultants and researchers' from the north, but it will also put these positions to debate with what they perceive to be the 'local knowledge' regarding the positions.

3.4 Given the post-cold war realities, the 'usefulness' of East Africa to the world is dwindling. It is in this context that some of the East African states have been referred to as 'failed states' or 'junk nations'. What is observable though is that despite the fact that this position has affected levels of aid and development assistance to the region, an East African response to this thinking is yet to emerge. The opportunity for SAREAT here is therefore to develop an *East African position* regarding East African politics. This we hope to do by i) putting to debate existing knowledge on politics and social order in the region as perceived by the northern knowledge engineers; ii) publishing and popularising locally generated research work on democratic transition in the region; and iii) creating a forum in which the East Africans can seize the initiative of setting the socio-economic and democratic reform agenda.

4. Strategies

SAREAT strategies within the New Africa Initiative are twofold

4.1 Institutional strategies
4.2 Programmatic and Product strategies

4.1 Institutional Strategies

4.1.1 Overall Strategy:

To create an institutional setting for innovative thinking that is loose enough to allow for flexibility and for some trial and error but well rationalised to ensure that lessons learnt from this experimentation are incorporated into broad institutional objectives and programmes.

4.1.2 Specific Strategy

4.1.2.1 **Mobilisation:** This is the process of translating the *idea into practice.* We hope to mobilise talent from both the accomplished and upcoming scholars. We also hope to mobilise financial and material resources from as diversified a group of donors as possible.

4.1.2.2 **Coalition-building:** SAREAT intends to build a network of 'support systems' drawn from the universities world-wide, non-governmental research organisations, civil society formations, the other NAI partners and any other organisations whose activities will contribute to our work.

4.1.2.3 **Creating Stake holders:** SAREAT hopes to create its own stake holders in the form of subscribers, partners (providing material and financial support), and, in the long run, members. These will provide us with feed-back from our 'clients'.

4.2 Programme and Product Strategies

Our programme and product strategies work towards the realisation of the institutional objectives set out in the section on opportunities. SAREAT shall have two programmes which include a) publishing and b) research, in that order of importance. Our research activities shall focus primarily on issues of governance and the democratic transition in the region.

Our publishing programme shall have three products

- 4.2.1 Book Series
- 4.2.2 Journal of East African Alternatives
- 4.2.3 East African Alternatives - A monthly Review of Political Economy in East Africa

4.2.1 Book Series

We shall publish books based on research work done in East Africa by East Africans. These books shall be in the areas of politics of transition and democratisation in the region. Two books are expected by the end of October (dummies are available). The first one is on *Constitution-Making and the Crisis of the Nation-State in Kenya* edited by Mutahi Ngunyi and Wachira Maina. The book has 14 chapters which have been produced by a group of researchers working from the Institute of Policy Analysis and Research (IPAR) and funded by the Ford Foundation. The second book is a product of some collaborative work between the same group of researchers and the Department of Politics at the University of Leeds. It is entitled *Aid and the Democratic Transition in Kenya* edited by Mutahi Ngunyi and Lionel Cliffe. This volume will be jointly released by SAREAT and the Centre for Democratisation at Leeds University.

We hope to release another three books in the first quarter of 1998. Two of these are funded by the Ford Foundation at IPAR while one is from the on-going work at the University of Nairobi supported by the Africa Association of Political Scientists (AAPS).

4.2.2 Journal of East African Alternatives

This will be a quarterly journal which will publish articles sourced from East African researchers and peer reviewed internationally. The quarters shall include November 1997, February, May and August 1998. The premier issue of the Journal is expected to be out in November 1997.

4.2.3 East African Alternatives - A Monthly Review of Political Economy in East Africa

This is a monthly magazine with contributors drawn from the academia, civil society formations, popular media and from development and political practitioners. It will differ from the existing set of magazines in East Africa in that it will do a comparative analysis of the politics of the region on a monthly basis. This analysis shall also be done by contributing editors in the areas we shall be examining.

7. Outreach Strategy

7.1. The gap the publications hope to fill

There are numerous publications in East Africa. These fall into two broad categories. The first are the publications produced by academic and non-governmental policy institutions, issue-based professional associations and international/regional organisations situated in the region. Such publications include the *Urban Quarterly, Eco-News, The Jurist,* and *Working (*or *Discussion) Papers* of such institutions as the Centre for Basic Research (CBR) in Uganda, Institute for Development Studies (IDS) and the African Centre for Technology and Science (ACTS) in Kenya.

Most of these publications are country-specific. The existing regional publications in this category have either wound up like the *East African Journal* did following the collapse of the East African Community. Apart from publications by Claripress which are regional in their reach, most of the other existing ones are 'unhealthy' publications which are released sporadically. Even then, such publications have a limited circulation.

None of the publications in this category in East Africa focus on the political economy of the region.[10] Those that examine political economy issues are country specific and lack a comparative angle. This is not to say that they have not been useful in the analysis of the political situation in East Africa. Publications from CBR, ACTS and IDS have raised pertinent country-specific political economy issues that have a bearing on the other countries of the region. Because of poor marketing systems in the region, both the readership and circulation of these publications is low.[11]

The second category of publications are of the general public type. These are basically news-oriented and fall into different categories. There are the daily newspapers like the *Nation, the East African Standard,* the *New Vision* and the *Monitor* with a regional readership, and the *East African, Indian Ocean*

[10] This is with the exception of Claripress publications. These are however not irregular in their production.

[11] We hope to lay emphasis on the marketing of the journal in order to ensure that it reaches our target audience.

Newsletter, and the *Africa Analysis* which do news analysis. Being news-oriented publications, they provide the most updated profile of the democratic transition in East Africa. But like all such publications, they do not provide a detailed analysis of the news and other 'non-news' developments in the region that have a bearing on the process of transition.

The Journal of East African Alternatives hopes to be a hybrid of these two types of publications. It is intended to be readable and current, well-researched, innovative. provocative and empirical. *The Monthly Review of Political economy in East Africa* will be a much lighter product. It is hoped to have a creative flair, to develop a reputation for leadership in quality, and to be competitive in price.

7.2 Target Readers and Audiences

Within East Africa, the SAREAT publications will be read by different categories of people.

7.2.1 Progressive Bureaucrats

They will be interested in understanding the policy environment in which they operate. We hope to have this provided for by the new social movements and the new economic formations from whom we shall draw the information.

The audiences of these bureaucrats include the politicians in government who have "no time" to read journal articles[12], but who rely on the technocrats for information, policy design and implementation. Arguably, 'consumers' of these policies are also audiences of the bureaucrats in the sense that the policies affecting them will hopefully be influenced by the journal articles, the books and the magazine.

7.2.2 Civil Society Actors

Given the fast-changing nature of the issues tackled by civil society formations the SAREAT publications will be useful as a tool that updates them on new advocacy techniques, practices and issues.

The audiences of these actors include the general public, specific social categories like rural women, and members of these civil society groups (like associations or professional groups). The general public and specific social

[12] It must be noted here that the journal will be in a language that is friendly to the government politician. His/ her failure to read it should be purely out of lack of time or interest.

categories will benefit through civic and voter education programmes which will be influenced by the journal articles. They will also benefit indirectly through advocacy, activism and publications done by civil society groups.

As for the new social movements (mainly development NG0s), their audiences are the development consumers who benefit from these movements' programmes of social provisioning and training.

7.2.3 Activist Organisations and Political Party Leadership

Both political parties and activist groups in East Africa are increasingly relying on scientifically generated information for their planning and drawing of strategies. The SAREAT publications will provide them with this kind of information in a readable and practical way. This will give them a map detailing the process of democratic transition not only in their specific countries, but in the other East African countries as well.

The audiences of political parties include the general public, and the government for those in the ruling party. Those of the activist organisations include institutions of government, and the beneficiaries of the activities of these organisations.

7.2.4 Donor Agencies and Missions

Discourse in these institutions is largely informed by non-resident East Africanists. The SAREAT publications will provide these institutions with a local perspective regarding the issues they make policies about. This perspective will be presented by those working on the 'policy site' that concern these institutions. This should make the SAREAT publications a useful policy-making tool.

The audiences of these institutions include the government ministries they negotiate with, the home governments/agencies they report to and the public sector they interact with through grant-making.

7.2.5 Corporate Actors

These are becoming increasingly interested in the political environment they operate in. They will find the SAREAT publications, especially the journal, a detailed source of analysis regarding the changing politics of the region to supplement their other readings. Because of the nature of their operations, these actors have limited audiences beyond their corporate world.

7.2.6 The Media

Given the nature of the media industry, actors involved in news analysis have little time to do meaningful research. Lack of accurate background information, or necessary facts about a situation has in many cases resulted in inaccurate analysis with far reaching effects. The media will use the SAREAT publications as a reference material on issues of political reforms in East Africa. The fact that the publications will be research-based, analytical and empirical, makes them useful sources of information.

The general public is the audience for the media. Policy makers and other strategic actors also constitute part of the media audience through columns aimed at quality reach. Positions taken in the journal should find their way to some of these columns through the media actors.

7.2.7 The Academics (Local and International)

The academics will be interested in the journal because they have to keep abreast of changing patterns and emerging issues in the process of political reforms in the region. They will also find it useful as a source of raw empirical data from different sectors of society. For the international scholars, the SAREAT publications will be useful in that it will provide them with a multi-faceted[13] 'ground picture' of the process of transition in East Africa. The local scholars will find this a useful forum for disseminating their research findings and engaging the internationally generated knowledge on East Africa.

The audiences of these scholars are numerous. These include students at the Universities and research institutes, colleagues in seminars and conferences, and most importantly, the clientele for whom they do consultancy work locally and internationally. Most development agencies and donor organisations depend on these actors for consultations on diverse areas of reform strategy and policy.

7.3 Sample Table of Issues to be Handled in the Journal[14] and the Monthly

7.3.1 Constitution-making, Competing Ethnicities and the Question of Citizenship

- The Asian Question
- The racial question in the politics of the union in Tanzania

---

[13] Multi-faceted because it is presented by actors from different sectors of society.
[14] These issues will be refined and contributors identified after a visit to the three countries of the region.

- The citizenship question:
  (in northern Uganda-Ugandans of Sudanese origin; in Kenya - Kenyans of British, Somali and Ethiopian (Oromo) origin).
- Ethnic citizenship and constitution-making[15]

7.3.2 Cultural Nationalism and Internal Conflict

- War in Northern Uganda
- Ethnic/land clashes in Kenya
- The Tanganyika/Zanzibari question
- Crisis in the Great Lakes Region and its bearing on East Africa

7.3.3 Changing patterns of Foreign Intervention in East Africa

- Changing forms of foreign investment
  (East Asian and South African capital influx)
- Changing foreign interests - from strategic to commercial interests (French 'invasion' of East Africa after Rwanda, Japanese and German increasing presence in the region)
- Aid as a tool for the promotion of human rights and democracy
- Changing tools of aid engineering
  (from negative to positive conditionality)

7.3.4 The Different Faces of Civil Society in East Africa

- The differentiated nature of civil society
- The contest between the state sector, popular sector and the 'Institutionalised' sector of civil society. (Mainly in Kenya and Tanzania)
- Changing roles of development NG0s under political liberalisation
- An assessment of the democracy and governance sector of civil society

7.3.5 Electoral Politics and the Crisis of Democratic Transition

- A comparative analysis of the multi-party/no-party elections in East Africa
- The political economy of the electoral process
  (impact of economic liberalisation on electioneering)
- Foreign Interests and Electoral Politics
  (conflicting foreign interests on electoral process etc.)

---

[15] Interesting works on this issue have been done by Prof. Steve Ndegwa of the College of William and Mary, and Prof. Mamdani in various publications.

- Regime re-invention and electoral politics

7.4 Marketing Strategies

For purposes of ensuring that the distribution of the SAREAT publications covers as many geographical areas as possible, we shall have numerous points of distribution world-wide. Such points include M. Heins in North America (currently distributing a number of African journals), distributors in Europe - possible explorations with mainly the Nordic Africa Institute (NAI), the Norwegian Institute of Human Rights, and distribution firms in India, and the Southern part of Africa. Distribution in the other parts of Africa will be done from Nairobi.

We have already developed a mailing list of 11,000 universities and institutions of higher learning world-wide with the help of the UNESCO office in Nairobi. These form part of the target market we hope to 'capture'. An aggressive marketing strategy will be developed for each product.

8. The Vision of SAREAT

The principal vision of SAREAT is to rebuild the local knowledge industry. The key approach to this is to indigenize research. And we expect that this will lead to the resuscitation of civic society in East Africa.

Discussion and Exchange of Views

This presentation led to an extended and animated discussion. A whole series of issues were raised in connection with publication and with materials to be published. For instance, the first issue that was raised was the perennial problem of weighing between quality of research and quantity of publications. A balance must be stricken between the two so as to ensure the publication of quality material. It was suggested that care must be taken to maintain balance between the empirical and the conceptual (or even the theoretical) in the publications. Concern was expressed that empirical material may dominate to the detriment of conceptual and theoretical writings. The kind of language that should be used as a medium for the publications in view of the objective of reaching a wider mass (both rural and urban) was the other problem aired in the course of the exchange of views. How this audience can be reached was the other related problem which was addressed to the presenters. One person from the floor wondered what in the first place is meant by indigenizing policy debates and where the dividing line could fall between international and local knowledge.

The other set of issues aired and discussed concerned SAREAT itself. How is it organized? Does it have the required size to fulfill the task that it has set for itself? What is its legal status? These and other similar issues were raised and discussed at length. Numerous suggestions were forwarded to the presenters.

6

MUSEUMS, ETHNICITY AND DEMOCRACY: A Proposal for a Project - The National Museums of Kenya

Mohamed Isahakia[*]

1. Introduction

The proposal covers a 3 year programme of activities designed to facilitate the National Museums of Kenya's (NMK) role in establishing a partnership with local communities to revive traditional knowledge on conflict resolution. The proposed budget is US$250,000.00. The programme will focus on developing the regional Museums as forums for cultural dialogue among different ethnic communities. Key activities will include training in traditional conflict resolution, use of indigenous knowledge information for wider advocacy on key issues affecting the scope of peace in the region and enhancing the recognition of traditional elders as peace makers at community level. Through the shared experience of developing community based multi-ethnic exhibits on traditional conflict management in the Museums, local communities will be encouraged to work closely among themselves. These activities aimed at utilization of cultural resources as a basis for promoting ethnic harmony will allow the Museum to assume a more prominent role in nation building by educating and mobilizing the local communities to minimize conflict while making new choices.

2. Background

Ethnic conflict and democratisation emerged as two major trends in politics in the world upon the end of the cold war. After its role as an arena of cold war conflict came to an end, global attention to Africa is awakened mostly by famine relief or a sudden cross border refugee crisis. Yet Africa continues to

[*] Director General, National Museums of Kenya.

demonstrate a range of political vectors with regard to ethnicity and democratic trends in politics which are no less challenging than in other parts of the world. The spectrum of political manoeuvrings of the past few years in African countries illustrates, not unexpectedly, ambivalence in dealing with ethnicity in an open and competitive political arena. Governments demonstrate wide divergence: the urge towards abolition on the one hand and group representation on the other. But the spectrum also spans positions in between: the attempt to overcome ethnic division by banning expression of ethnicity in politics, the practice of representing ethnic groupings when faced with the necessities of governance, the fear of ethnic domination by other groups or groups with monarchical status, the rewarding of ethnic group supporters, and the manipulation of ethnic connection as a ticket to power.

As politics becomes more open, each of these trends spawns opposing forces as well. These opposing forces call into question any general trend towards the installation and consolidation of democratic governments. One of the main obstacles to nation building in Africa in general has been internal ethnic conflict which not only threatens national unity but also frustrates and retards economic and social development. Consequently in many African countries a fundamental issue today is whether nationhood remains a viable concept at all.

The urgent need is to develop a formula that can politically, economically, socially and culturally utilize the values and institution of traditional societies (which we subsume under the label of indigenous knowledge) by recognizing them and building on them in a manner that reconciles these societies and makes them partners with the forces of modern science and technology. Many African countries have rejected ethnicity as an organizing concept in the process of nation building. The challenge to many cultural institutions then is whether it is possible to reverse the mindset so that ethnicity which is an African reality can be seen as a resource or a building block that can provide a sound foundation for sustainable political and socio-economic development from within.

2.1 Ethnicity and Conflict Reconciliation: Role of Museums

Africa today is facing a crisis of immense proportions as democracy and the quest for pluralism has unleashed ethnic consciousness in the minds of many Africans. This crisis in one way or another reflects the apparently conflicting needs to build a global society in which all ethnic groups can participate while preserving specific cultural values and identities.

Museums are products of their social context and it is proper that they should be so. If we accept then that their purpose is to be of service to society, then it is vital that they be responsive to their social environment in order to remain relevant to changing social needs and goals. Changing social environments in Africa demands that Museums that used to be historically eurocentric in their outlook henceforth need to foster the systematic inclusion of diverse cultural elements in their interpretive and educational activities. If Museums in Africa can make this cultural shift, they could have the opportunity to do even more than continuing to be only centres for the exchange of cultural ideas. They can have the potential for assuming a new role that ascends to an extremely new plane - to become more pivotal to the continuing evolution of culture and to be genuine instruments of cultural reconciliation that African society so desperately needs. Part of this shift involves transferring Museums from being temples for an elite which enjoys the status of a privileged caste into a place that fosters multicultural dialogue.

Culture is central to conflict (and therefore to conflict resolution) as well as to development both by determining the identity of the peoples involved as groups and individuals and by shaping the techniques and mechanisms that they evolved over a long period. It is in this area that Museums can play a crucial role in serving as fora for discussion and exchange of cultural ideas among different ethnic groups.

Encouraging the mutual recognition of cultural differences is therefore a major challenge for our Museums. Exhibitions that are cross-cultural have a tremendous potential to inform the community about themselves by setting their culture and history side by side with others.

In a multi-ethnic society such as Kenya the problem facing a national museum such as NMK is to reflect an identity that has a national validity yet one that is relevant to all individual ethnic groups. NMK's hope therefore is that through acquiring an understanding of other cultures, all Kenyans will appreciate the inner logic of social systems that are different from their own and hence develop an appreciation and respect for them that will combat prejudices. Mutual appreciation and co-operation among the cultural groups that make up Kenyan society is seen as the necessary foundation for Kenya to remain a single nation in the face of democratic change.

3. Key Issues to be Addressed by NMK

The NMK believes that a rich culture constitutes a cornerstone in a vital democratic system. Every society is stimulated and enriched by, and dependent on, the fact that humanistic and creative forces have the opportunity to live, survive and develop. Creative thought is needed to find unconventional solutions in situations of chaos and conflict. Culture can have many missions in the process of democratisation; for example to build bridges between different groups; to put forth peace aspiration and reconciliation; and to heal traumatized minds. Cultural experiences infuse the will to live and provide an opportunity to treat traumatized experiences.

These are some essential ingredients in efforts to strengthen civic society as an important part in a vital democracy. Museums as social institutions are a potential force in forging consciousness within specific historical contexts and as part of a political process of democratization. As national legacy, their collections can promote national identities and common national agenda. As part of a national agenda, their objects stand for nation state and embody the "idea" of the state for a people - for example the Old Testament for Israel. They are spaces in which elites and competing social groups express their ideas and views. Unlike churches and other public institutions, there is no hereditary or ordained monopoly of access, possession and display of symbols of power. On the contrary, museums accommodate diverse contents and ideas. Access is tolerated and even encouraged among a large and differential population making accumulated knowledge widely available.

The focus of this project is to use the Museum as a forum to discuss the values and institutions of traditional societies (indigenous knowledge and culture) in the process of democratisation and sustainable development. It is hoped that this project will facilitate the role of Museums in promoting cross-cultural understanding, participatory and sustainable approaches to democratic development and the realization that indigenous knowledge systems represent a critical resource base for the process of building nationhood.

NMK has therefore several functions relevant to the project under discussion:

1. Develop partnerships with all communities in documenting and preserving their cultural heritage.
2. Promote public education on the role of multi-culturalism in nationhood.
3. Make museums a common-ground for all communities to be represented.

4. Project Aims and Objectives

The overall strategy is to make relevant the role of culture in promoting cross-cultural understanding and therefore peace and harmony through the medium of musuems. In particular NMK aims to support and consolidate traditional cultural components that can be made part of decisions for national economic and political development and to establish understanding of the significance of material culture and indigenous knowledge and their arrangement and use in museums as the embodiment and reflection of the accumulated knowledge and values of nationhood.

Therefore the intention is to promote African cultural components as tools for decision making for national economic and political development taking into account what is indigenous and useful. For example traditional institutions of leadership have for long regulated successfully relations between those exercising authority and influence and the governed. African judicial processes have traditionally stressed equity and reconciliation as opposed to confrontation and the assignment of blame which is a characteristic of western legal systems.

Our concerns as a Museum are then to suggest answers to the following questions:

1. What are ethnic conflicts in the traditional sense?
2. How have these conflicts been resolved or managed?
3. How can multi-ethnicity become an asset to the developments of democracy in Kenya?

In finding answers to these questions, the NMK will undertake the following activities.

4.1 Build Capacity of the NMK to Establish a Role in the Democratisation Process

In the effort to consolidate the role of NMK as a forum for promoting public advocacy on the subject of Culture, Ethnicity and Democracy, the Museum intends to host a two day workshop that will bring together local communities, NGO'S, civic institutions, religious organizations, museologists, social and cultural anthropologists, politicians and people from the local administration.

The workshop will have five main objectives:

1. To facilitate effective communication and collaboration between different ethnic communities by using the Museum and its collections to illuminate ethnic cultures and create mutual respect;
2. To develop collaboration and collective efforts between institutions, organizations and people involved in conflict resolution;

3. To allow debate on the question of ethnicity as a global issue and draw examples from other experiences where ethnicity and multi-culturalism has become a critical resource for nation building;
4. To galvanize practical action amongst cultural institutions and agencies to address ethnicity and causes of conflict; and
5. To give prominence to the role of indigenous knowledge systems in the democratisation process.

4.2 Build Effective Community Linkages and Advocacy for Democracy

NMK will also seek to bring together different communities to work on the theme of Traditional Conflict Resolution Management by providing a forum at the regional level.

This project will have several objectives:

1. Through research develop a clear vision for peace and conflict resolution based on the understanding of the cultural dimension of conflict amongst different communities.
2. Increase the recognition of the role of traditional elders, healers and women in conflict resolution.
3. Enhance the diffusion of tension in social relations through organising exhibitions jointly with communities on cross-ethnic conflict resolution practices. Here the communities themselves will participate in the collection and documentation of material culture used in the context of conflict resolution. These will be augmented by visual documentation of traditional practices of conflict resolution and management.
4. Provide significance to peace sites through the gazettment and protection of such sites as important national cultural monuments. The Museum will then allow the communities to manage these sites.
5. Document events which celebrate peace work among and between communities.
6. NMK will undertake efforts to revitalise traditional skills of conflict resolution and management through:

   6.1 Training of 'trainers' around key peace making skills to complement community workers.

6.2 Participation in joint work with other institutions and organizations to discuss issues relating to national peace and development.

7. Include Administration officials (Chiefs, Police, District Administration) in understanding and addressing traditional values in mediating peace among different ethnic groups.

4.3 Establishing and Building Links Between African Museums and Other Institutions

One of the main purposes of the project is to increase, what we call, NMK Community Voluntary Action in order to encourage a strong culture of tolerance and responsibility for social harmony. NMK believes that this depends upon developing a practical approach to the building of linkages between regional museums, local communities and key institutions to increase the scope for conveying community needs to the general public and policy makers in particular.

In order to achieve this the NMK will aim to bring together NGO's, religious organizations and local communities. This will provide experience for other communities and public officials throughout Kenya. Such experience will also be available to other regional Museums within East and Central Africa. Through information and communication work, it is also intended that the experience of NMK will be of active interest to international organizations involved in peace. Some of the institutions envisaged to take part in this work are the Global Network of Indigenous Resource Centres, (IKC), and Museums both in Africa, Europe and North America. We are pleased to announce that they have also expressed interest in the Project.

6.1 Democracy and Conflict Prevention and Resolution

Sultan H. Somjee
Division of Ethnography
National Museums of Kenya

The NMK addressed three areas of concern within the parameters outlined by the goals of New African Initiative. These are social concerns pertaining to ethnicity, religion and race.

In the area of ethnicity we have been working with twelve pastoralist groups and more recently we have initiated work among three agriculturalist groups. The focus has been on learning about and strengthening cultures of peace of the various groups rather than attempting to solve present crises. The East African Cultures of Peace have been overlooked if not ignored by academics as well as by the governments, NG0s and the media. Yet this unacknowledged resource of indigenous knowledge is the counterpart of a tradition that also gives rise to ethnic conflicts. Looking at the other side of the coin has been our approach. Our purpose as a museum is to explore and give greater exposure to the positive image of Africa, to challenge the warrior image and promote dialogue, democracy and peace.

The second concern relates to dialogue and understanding between different faiths and especially between Christianity and Islam. There is untapped potential in religious understanding and tolerance for appreciation and practice of good relationships, among the diversities of beliefs and values cherished by East African societies.

The third concern that the NMK addressed has been the history and representation of non-indigenous cultures in East Africa whose presence has been here for several centuries. The differences of racial, religious and cultural backgrounds have created suspicion and uneasiness that easily lead to tension and violence. The focus of concern has been Asian Africans, whose ancestral roots like those of African Americans, are in one continent but their homeland is in another continent.

The three concerns create situations of social ill feelings that are sometimes manipulated and escalated by complexities of national and international politics and business interests. The NMK working within its mandate of research, collection, documentation, training and public education initiated programmes that address the three concerns at both the academic and community levels.

The following are the specific results of our activities:

1. Research

Dr. Somjee is currently working among several ethnic communities comprising both the pastoralist and agriculturalist groups. The focus of his research is on understanding concepts, rituals and artifacts associated with reconciliation processes. Our initiative has laid a foundation for further research which will enhance the resources of the Division of Ethnography and open up new areas related to democracy and reconciliation from view points of different social structures. The research out-put has drawn the attention of

NGOs, the UN and other bodies to the relevance of African indigenous modes of conflict resolution.

Two other areas that are currently researched are Cultures of Peace of Muslim Societies and Asian African Cultures of Eastern Africa. The following paragraphs on Workshops, Exhibitions and Public Education, Training and Capacity Building, Publications and Documentation elaborate on the outcome of the initial work which constitutes actually fundamental research for establishing the direction for developing our component of New African Initiatives.

2. Workshops

Two workshops were held this year. *Confluences of Peace Traditions* (Nairobi: March, 1998) had a participation of twenty five pastoralists representing eight ethnic groups. The workshop was held at National Museums of Kenya for five days and it included a field trip to a Maasai area where there is a collection of peace artifacts. The format of the workshop was such that the different groups exchanged their views and traditions and peace building experiences.

The second workshop was on *Cultures of Peace of Muslim Societies* which was held in September this year. This was a one day forum where discussions on the practice of peace were shared among five different Islamic groups. The Somali group included five clans. (See Appendix I).

This forum turned out to be timely and well prepared. There is a general feeling of uneasiness among Muslims in Kenya following the Nairobi bomb blast and de-registration of Islamic NG0s. The discussions were well received and participated.

Dr. Somjee attended the International symposium on Culture of Peace in Germany in August this year. He gave a slide presentation on the East African research experience and outcome of the Museum's project. As a follow-up, Dr. Somjee is now invited to make a case for an East African Peace Museum at the International Conference of Peace Museums in Osaka, Japan in November this year[1998].

3. Exhibition and Public Education

We assembled an exhibition of some 200 artifacts used in reconciliation rituals and other non-ritual objects of material culture that are respected by various public communities as symbols of their peace making traditions.

We invited artists from Nairobi to study and reflect on them and present their conclusions in painting and sculptures. Thirty artists, mainly of agricultural backgrounds, participated in the exhibition. There were awards for the best artworks which were judged by pastoralist representatives whose peace traditions were being exhibited.

Nairobi Museum records show that about 80,000 visitors passed through the exhibition entitled *Heritage of Peace* and *Reconciliation* between March and August, 1998. We received hundreds of very encouraging comments. Many were written down in the visitor's books. (Appendix II for some samples of comments).

Dr. Somjee also gave a number of lectures on Indigenous Modes of Conflict Resolution.

4. Training and Capacity Building

Dr. Somjee has been guiding postgraduate students of anthropology to pursue studies in Peace Heritage of ethnic groups, Islamic Peace Cultures in Eastern Africa and Asian African Studies. He has supervised three students at Masters level in each one of these areas. Two students have succeeded in getting places at reputable universities in England. One of them recently left to study at the University of London. (MA proposals see Appendix III).

5. Publications

A book *Honey and Heifer, Grasses, Milk and Water: A Heritage of Diversity in Reconciliation* compiled and edited by Dr. Somjee, was launched in March, 1999 at the Nairobi National Museum. About 300 people from all walks of life - ambassadors, NGO personnel, ethnic people, professionals and lay people attended the launch and the opening of the accompanying exhibition. Since then we have been receiving many positive comments and requests for more information on the project.
There have been five newspaper and magazine articles on the research and public education work undertaken by the National Museums of Kenya with reference to Conflict Resolution. (Appendix IV).

6. Documentation

The Ford Foundation funding has enabled us to document the project activities and Reconciliation Workshops in great detail. This has become a tremendous resource material for future work for academic, public and school education. The Division of Ethnography has produced ethnographic study materials in conjunction with the Audio-Visual Department of the National

Museums of Kenya. The anthropological material in the following six categories reflects the diversity of cultural perspectives on conflict resolution and its great potential for guiding future activities :

Category 1

Video recordings of the workshops include:

Kitale *Peace and Conflict Resolution* meeting where ten ethnic groups shared their concerns and experiences relating to conflicts.

Nairobi *Peace of Conflict Resolution* meeting which was attended by twenty five ethnic participants.

Cultures of Peace of Muslim Societies, a forum where representatives of five different Islamic community's participated.

Category II

Rituals of Reconciliation opening ceremony at the exhibition.

Category III

Ethnography programme especially produced for school and public education

Osotua - Maasai Peace story
Mis - Pokot Peace Story
Ekisitli - Turkana Peace Story

KBC, Africa Journal (Reuters) and BBC have shown interest in using these productions and other footage material.

Category IV

Filming of actual ceremonies in the field in Kajiado and Narok District.

Category V

Photographs and slides

We have a collection of approximately 300 images of our research and workshop activities on Reconciliation and Peace in Eastern Africa.

Category VI

Material Culture Collection

Approximately 200 peace and reconciliation artifacts have been documented. For the broad society that is non-literate, material culture embodies wisdom, knowledge and traditions that cannot be expressed otherwise by the people. We are now working on a museum catalogue to publish this collection which is probably the first African collection of peace artifacts. (Appendix V on this section is prepared by Mr. Kimotho, Audio-Visual Department).

CONCLUSION

The Museum has approached the New African Initiative Project at two levels. One is the level of academia which has resulted in publications, workshops and training of graduates. In all, this has greatly enhanced the capacity of the Division of Ethnography. The other level addresses public awareness and education. This has resulted in public exhibitions, school progammes, media articles and public lectures.

The project focuses on three concerns which have been the subject of research and subsequent activities. The concerns pertain to issues of ethnicity, race and religion. A vast body of material, knowledge and experiences accumulated by the project during the year presents strong evidence for a need to establish an African Peace Museum. Most significantly, an African Peace Museum would promote and show how Africans have historically handled their own conflicts and in that it would contribute towards World Peace Traditions.

DISCUSSION AND EXCHANGE OF VIEWS (NMK)

Participants enquired into the capacity of the Museum to undertake the project particularly if it involves research. Moreover, it was asked whether chiefs and other traditional community leaders could be used in the process of cultural development and preservation of natural heritage as well as in the democratisation process. The presenters were also asked whether or not communities participated in the formulation of the project. The question of the role of the youth was raised in several forms- the most important form being that of accessibility of museums to students in both the formal and informal educational processes. Last but not least was the query that was related to the very substance of the presentation: how could museums help in the resolution and management of conflict?

To all these questions satisfactory responses were given. There was a rich and diverse discussion which, it was hoped by participants, would help in the enrichment of the project.

7

CONTRIBUTIONS OF THE MEDIA TO THE NEW AFRICAN INITIATIVE - Development Through Media

Dommie Yambo-Odotte

1. Introduction

Development Through Media (DTM) is a registered non-profit making organization. The organization's main focus is the effective utilization of the media as a tool for the dissemination of critical issues on social development in East Africa. DTM also aims at collaborating with media organizations from other parts of the world in its development and thus establish itself as a key component to the growth of a vibrant film industry in East Africa.

This is particularly important because much time and money continue to be spent by several organizations on development work in East Africa. These works have included research work on gender, health and socio-economic development among others. These works must be allowed to transcend their current preserve- that of the elite who have tended often to present information in esoteric ways which are at times not accessible to ordinary people. DTM wants to present itself as the bridge between the elite and the ordinary people, by presenting the same information in highly entertaining and moving media formats attractive to wide and diverse audiences.

2. DTM's Role in the New African Initiative

Ordinary people in East Africa do not engage in the debate on democracy, human rights and good governance at the global level where the pressure to be familiar with a host of international conventions is very high. Ordinary people deal with these issues of human rights, democracy and good governance in very ordinary ways. It is out of these ordinary experiences that basic freedoms, rights and obligations are given grassroots meaning, a meaning which enables nurturing of good governance from a firm empirical foundation: where the people are.

Ordinary people were already struggling for a better life and better society long before the ushering in of multi party democracy and the defeat of apartheid. Tanzanians started making sacrifices not only for their own country but also for the liberation of South Africa. This part of the story is not often told.

Somehow, there is a need to tell the story of social transformation in East Africa in a way that balances the old with the new. Above all, the story should balance elite concerns and experiences with those of ordinary people. This is what DTM proposes to do. It is this realization that inspired DTM's current project, a 35 mm feature film dealing with East Africa's contribution to the rise of a new Africa of which I will tell you more later. In a significant but so far unrecognized way, the sacrifices made by ordinary East Africans for the struggle to end apartheid was and remains part and parcel of the struggle for democracy and good governance in East Africa itself, a struggle which will have great bearing on the rise of a New Africa.

3. Key Leadership Development Challenges

Like the defeat of colonialism, one party rule and Apartheid in the 20th century, the development of the mass media in Africa has not been smooth sailing. Visual media in Africa was not controlled by Africans until the 60s when Africans began to achieve independence. Unfortunately, the independence of African states did not bring about much change, either. The independence of African states did not necessarily usher in economic and cultural independence. Indeed, the electronic media in East Africa as in most parts of Africa became an instrument for the consolidation of power instead of being used as an integral arm of the socio-political and economic infrastructure serving useful development purposes. Instead, it has been used as an ordinary bureaucratic machine.

Doubtless, audio-visual production is an important component of mass media. It is a medium by which society can be informed, educated, enlightened and entertained. How it is handled and for what purpose it is put to use, will determine and reflect the way we view ourselves as a society and consequently, how we let others view us. For many years, there has been talks about the utilization of African talent within the region for the establishment of a vibrant and independent mass media industry. This, however, has been difficult despite the fact that East Africa is rich with beautiful natural and man made scenery, well trained and experienced audio-visual technical and production crew, as well as human interest stories suitable for a flourish industry. Because of this, many a tale of great people, great issues and great emerging nations have remained out of the lime-light to the detriment of both the emergence of a viable mass media industry, and the dissemination of critical information and ideas to support a broad process of socio-economic and democratic reforms in the three East African countries.

4. DTM: Opportunities to Make Critical Changes

The mass media development in Africa however has not been all together stagnant. In the recent years there has been new developments which has seen the setting up of independent radio and television stations around the continent. Unfortunately, some of these stations have developed with some colonial hung-ups. Many audio-visual production personnel have remained as appendages of Western media whose productions often do not represent Africa from an African perspectives. They have tended to continue portraying developments in Africa in a way they believe the West would like to see them - the bizarre, the extraordinary.

DTM thus realises the need for change and the desire to create a new generation of film makers who can produce audio-visual products from an East African and African point of view. This new generation of film makers will want to deal with social messages in interesting ways which can appeal to wide and diverse audiences in very special ways. These audio-visual products, while entertaining, will also educate audiences as well as popularize concepts of the New Africa initiative.

Because of the way politics has been presented in the past, audiences have tended to be turned off by political programmes. This has left them in very compromised positions. This apathy has kept them away from information which can allow them to play active roles in the developments taking place in East Africa. A new generation of film makers can deal with socio-political messages in interesting ways. They will make political programmes in less boring ways which can allow audiences to laugh about politics thereby removing it finally from its socio taboo status.

DTM also wishes to engage in discussions aimed at creating deliberate policies and selected issues to help in the training of young men and women in all aspects of audio-visual production; scripting, directing, acting etc, in order to have a constant creation of a new generation of film makers to keep at par with East Africa's and Africa's constant transformation.

DTM also believes that the current activities running within the New Africa Initiative namely Kituo cha Katiba, Uongozi School, Series of Alternative Research in East Africa Trust etc. must begin to transcend workshops like this one. The wider population in East Africa must begin to be drawn in. DTM proposes to begin serious media coverages in all aspects of the media as a way of drawing the wider masses into the Initiatives ideals. The setting up of the proposed East African audio-visual text facility will make this wish a reality.

5. Other Activities

Other DTM's proposed projects include the production of a television and radio programme entitled EAST AFRICA TODAY. This project also aims to establish an East Africa video, audio and text facility which will produce and disseminate socio-cultural information targeted at ordinary people's level in order to nurture a democratic public mind set in the region.

DTM also plans to establish training and research centres associated with media communication and related technical and practical skills.

6. Current Strategies

Audio-visual media can serve as a powerful tool of development since it's vivid, visual and interesting audio presentation can be suitable for both literate and illiterate audience.

It is this realization that inspired (as was pointed out above) DTM's current project, a 35 mm feature film dealing with East Africa's contribution to the rise of a new Africa. Excitement around the New South Africa remains as high today as it was when Nelson Mandela was sworn in as the first black South African President in 1994. The dismantling of apartheid will remain a monumental achievement in the 20th century, bearing testimony to the efficacy of collective human efforts and commitment to the fight against an injustice whose design was formulated in 1948, when the architects of apartheid found solace in the ideals of a system advocating for the apartness of races in "the spirit of good neighborliness"-black, white and coloured. The constitutionalization of apartheid was to remain in force for almost five decades there on.

For Africa, the apartheid system of Government was to add on to the many challenges facing the continent's struggle for survival and revival as it sought to set new standards to suit its development needs.

Although the defeat of apartheid remains one of the greatest human achievements in the fight against an institutionalized injustice in the 20th Century, it by no means indicates the end of the challenges that Africa must face in the next century as it continues to map out the course for its future.

This is contrary to the growing myth that the problems of colonialism, racism and dictatorship during the one party state era, the three problems which have deeply affected Africans will disappear with the turn of the century. This is particularly true with regards to the struggle against apartheid. The rise of the New South Africa, fuelled by the magic charm of Nelson Mandela, has given the impression that all the problems associated with the anti-apartheid struggle have been solved and now what remains is the process of reconstruction and development in South Africa. In other words, apartheid has been thought of primarily in terms of its impact within South Africa.

In effect, however, apartheid also meant part of the continent, and a re-imaging of South Africa within its continental setting. The victory of the democratic movement needs to transcend victory over the constitutional action that finally out-lawed apartheid. However, the pervasiveness of the ideology of apartheid has remained manifest in the retelling of the struggle against apartheid which continues to leave untold the contributions by ordinary people in the continent which made victory possible. In discussing Africa's continuing transformation, including the retelling of the success for the struggle which gave rise to the New South Africa, an important question to ask is who defines the New Africa, and who defines the agenda for that New Africa? Who designs the New democracy? Do East Africans have a role to play in defining the New Africa and in designing its agenda? But above all, what is the role of the ordinary people in all this? For ordinary people in South Africa who were separated from their sisters, brothers, sons, daughters, fathers and mothers, that place where they were, continues to remain beyond the realms of imagination. Where they lived, loved, started families and sometimes even died, has remained "unknown" as are the many children and loved ones left behind in the aftermath of the successful struggle against apartheid. It seems at times that remembering South Africa means forgetting the rest of Africa. Yet, the New South Africa owes much of its newness to sacrifices made by many African states, particularly Tanzania in the East African block in the successful fight against apartheid.

Let us remember here for a while that the battle to end apartheid was fought by many nations- rich and poor, developed and underdeveloped. On the African continent, some of the least resourced countries among them Tanzania, joined the battle at the fore-front with dire economic and social consequences. It is in these countries that many South Africans sought refuge from the pursuit of their country's police force and resided among ordinary people. Among these people, they found encouragement, support, love and warmth during those troubled times. At the dismantling of apartheid and the end of repatriation of former South African exiles back to South Africa in 1994, it became apparent through newspaper reports and individual interactions that something important was being omitted in the re-telling of the South African story. Thus, there arose a need to examine factors of human rights, democracy and good governance at a broad angle with the express aim of assessing the contribution and sacrifices made by East Africa, and by extension, other African countries towards the liberation of South Africa and the implications of the liberation struggle on their lives.

7. Civil Society Driven Research

It is against this background that DTM set to explore some of the silence within the mass media in order to indicate some of the ways and gaps in current knowledge, and suggest some of the gains that might be made from a civil society-driven research programme.

A first step was the total and complete understanding of the issues at hand. This required thorough research with visits to some selected African countries closely connected with the larger context of the story. Using East Africa as an entry point, the research process also embarked on the inventorying of historical and political facts from other countries like Zambia and South Africa in an attempt to present an overall African perspective.

This was done so that a clear picture could be achieved against which DTM would be able to come up with a media presentation that would enable the world to ask, act/or answer certain basic questions related to human rights, democracy and good governance as it relates to the successful dismantling of apartheid in South Africa.

Historical facts surrounding the contributions of African countries like Tanzania, Kenya, Uganda and Zambia towards the fight against apartheid are broadly known. As part of their commitment to fight against apartheid, many African leaders believed that no African state could consider themselves to be completely free if others were still in bondage. To this end, selfless commitment of the sometimes not so readily available resources towards the struggle, including the hosting of the freedom fighters in exile, was made. It is the geographical relocation of the exiled freedom fighters that was to have the greatest impact on the civil society in most of the host countries.

8. Apartheid: a Socio-Political Analysis

To fully appreciate the impact of the struggle against apartheid on ordinary people, a brief social-political analysis is necessary.

Support for the independence of other countries was something that T. A. N. U (Tanzania Africa Nation Union) leaders had inculcated in the thinking of Tanzanians even before independence. It became a tradition among the common people to support liberation movements. The ordinary citizens of Tanzania supported the South African liberation struggle both directly and indirectly. The government of Tanzania declared 1974 to be the YEAR OF LIBERATION. A liberation fund was started to intensify the struggle against oppression in South Africa to which people were asked to contribute generously. The ordinary citizens (to the surprise of the government) contributed selflessly. They gave whatever they could -food, grains(maize, wheat, millet, etc.) livestock (cattle, sheep, goat, donkeys) clothing and blankets. They donated countless pints of blood which was preserved especially for the fighters. Students from the university would have gone to fight if they had not been told to "Leave the fighting to the fighters concerned".

After the Sharperville Massacre, there was a mass exodus from South Africa. The refugees who came to Tanzania lived among the ordinary citizens. These contacts led to many sorts of marriages and the birth of many children. As a result of this, today there is a whole village(a little South Africa nicknamed Dark City by former South African refugees) near former Mazimbu camp in which live children born of South African fathers and the Tanzanian women who had relationships with them. The South African men have, since the liberation, gone back home. Peasants living around the refugee camps were displaced for the newly constructed camp's security reasons and also for their own security. The local people were often moved without compensation. This affected countless people living around the newly constructed camps like Kangwa, Mgagao, Mazimbu, Dakawa.

The Zambian story is very similar to Tanzania's. Her geographical position got her naturally involved in the South African struggle for liberation. It is no wonder then that A.N.C headquarters were based there. Many South Africans fled to Zambia both officially and unofficially. Those who came to Zambia unofficially had to depend on the goodwill of the ordinary citizens. Many of these citizens were already faced with painful structural adjustments caused by Zambia's decision to cut trade with South Africa. There were shortages of essential goods ranging from toilet paper to toothpaste. Despite all this, they accommodated the refugees and shared their limited resources willingly. The impact of the fight against apartheid was very great in Zambia. Many ordinary Zambians were killed by South African hit squads looking for A.N.C personalities believed, and rightly so, to be in hiding in that country.

The interaction between ordinary Zambians and the South African refugees led to large numbers of formal and informal marriages in which children were born. Today there are women and children in Zambia waiting for their husbands and fathers respectively who went back during the repatriation exercise. These husbands and fathers had promised to come back as soon as they were settled. The repatriation exercise started as early as 1990 and was officially closed in 1994. Mostly, there has been no news from the repatriated South Africans. Indeed, the Zambian women left behind continue to live a life of misery, while their children have formed a large part of the street children's population, unable to enjoy a dignified life with human rights concerns.

In Uganda, the South African liberation struggle was given moral rather than material support. Ordinary Ugandans identified with South African music which depicted the struggle against oppression. Students, peasants and workers related to revolutionary songs about Mandela. One story that hit headlines in South Africa recently is the story about a Ugandan boy who had travelled to South Africa in search of his adopted father. The story sparked off a lot of debate as it discussed a myriad other similar stories and, in particular, South Africa's treatment of immigrants. The story about the Ugandan boy searching for his father indicates that the kind of marriages that took place between South African freedom fighters and Tanzanian and Zambian women, was the modus operandi of the liberation struggle in large parts of Africa.

At the ordinary people's level, Kenya contributed to the struggle in various ways- most of them not measurable. More often than not, there is no documentation on the contributions made at the basic level either through individuals or non-governmental organizations. Many refugees who came to Kenya informally, were accommodated among the ordinary citizens. Universities offered them jobs while university students staged plays that castigated racial discrimination. They sang South African freedom songs to show solidarity with the blacks in South Africa. Nelson Mandela became a household name mainly because he represented the struggle. There is evidence that scholarships meant for Kenyan students were often re-channelled to benefit South African students. Many refugees from South Africa found shelter, food and clothing among ordinary Kenyans. Some entered into relationships in which children were born.

9. In the Aftermath of the Successful Struggle Against Apartheid

Given the above analysis, it is obvious that the struggle against apartheid created fertile grounds for socially explosive situations which are yet to be addressed. It should therefore follow that in the spirit of the reconstruction and development in South Africa the needs of ordinary people who were devastated by apartheid as a result of policies of governments which supported the anti-apartheid struggle in countries like Tanzania, Zambia, Angola, also needs to be taken into consideration through some deliberate process like the Truth and Reconciliation Commission of South Africa.

So far, there appears to be some conspiracy of silence about the fate of the victims of apartheid in some African countries. A notable group whose trials and tribulations after the end of legalized apartheid embodies important moral lessons for everyone concerned, are the women who had social and sexual relations with South African freedom fighters resident in countries like Tanzania during the anti-apartheid struggle. Many of these women ended up getting children out of the relationships. It appears now that the women and the children have become the **FORGOTTEN LOT** without proper homes and having difficulties making ends meet. But worse, the children only hear that they have South African fathers but they do not know where they are, or whether they are alive or dead. Tanzania has many such women and their children. The children have a crippling identity crisis, they think they are South Africans by descent but the South African government does not even acknowledge their existence, let alone entertain their claims to South African citizenship. The children are Tanzanian by birth but the Tanzanian government is not giving the same attention it gave to South African freedom fighters. Indeed, the children live in Tanzania like refugees in camps left by the South African freedom fighters. These children desperately need to have their human rights restored. They need to identify with a home but there is some controversy as to where home is: is home in Tanzania where they were born, or is home in South Africa from where their fathers came and where the fathers most probably are currently? And how about the mothers of these children? Don't they have human rights which are being violated by South African authorities and possibly Tanzanian authorities? This is an important question in view of the fact that many of the women have tried to trace their former "husbands" in South Africa only to be met with the brutal response of the lingering apartheid institutions, particularly among the police and immigration authorities. Many of the women are being held in South African jails or holding cells in disused mines. While the children are being held as refugees in Tanzania, the mothers are being held as refugees in South Africa.

10. Justification

Needless to say, the successful dismantling of apartheid is by no means a small achievement. The danger, however, lies in the possibility of overlooking human rights issues when momentarily blinded by the glare of great achievement. Granted, apartheid was one of the greatest problems that faced Africa in this century, putting many South Africans through some of the worst mental and physical anguish. It was therefore important that, at liberation, South Africa was to set upon a healing and reconciliation process that would allow new development and better racial interaction to take place. Under the circumstances, one might ask, why South Africa should be concerned with the issues surrounding the impact of apartheid outside South Africa at a time when South Africans themselves have yet to come to terms with the challenges in their own country upon the defeat of apartheid. However, another question might likewise be asked in an attempted response, when is a good time to raise the issue of the women and children, who because of their involvement in the struggle against apartheid, cannot today live a life of dignity as human beings? DTM contends that the time is now for later may be too late. The fate of these women calls to mind events years ago, in the period around the World War II when underaged Korean and Japanese women were forced into employment of servicing Japanese male soldiers? It took 40 years for that crime against humanity to come to the fore. But that was then. Today, near obsession with human rights concerns cannot permit the fate of the women and children victims of the apartheid struggle to be relegated to the back of a reconstruction and reconciliation process that is currently taking place in South Africa, and not least the democratization process currently taking place in East Africa and Africa as a whole.

11. The Need

It is important to appreciate that the Tanzanian and other African women who gave comfort to South African freedom fighters are human beings with human feelings and objectives in life. The children resulting from these liaisons must be allowed to live a full life which will prepare them better for their roles as future adults. Sadly, some of them may already have been lost to delinquent activities given the current vacuum in which they have been forced to live. There is a need, therefore, as a matter of urgency, to ensure that their current state of being is resolved as a matter of interest to East Africa, South Africa and indeed the world. DTM has thus proposed a feature film.

12. The Feature Film

That a good number of people in Africa who had contributed selflessly to the struggle against apartheid now find themselves on the opposite side of the success story is a foregone conclusion, that their current state remains 'unknown' is a serious human rights violation. Thus DTM has developed a feature film story for the production of a full length feature film which aims at helping audiences to begin to appreciate the contributions of African countries like Tanzania, Kenya and Uganda to the making of the New South Africa. Through a human interest love story, something that would make the story interesting and entertaining, it is hoped that this film will impact on the ongoing political liberalization and democratization in East Africa, as it would on the reconstruction process in South Africa, by raising the hitherto silent factors surrounding the effects of the antiapartheid struggle on these people. The proposed film will mobilize large and diverse audiences interested in positive change within civil society and national governance in East Africa and elsewhere in Africa. It is also hoped that the film's message may throw more light into the issue which may begin the process of solving the current situation of the women and children connected to South African freedom fighters. It is important that what is happening to the mothers and children be made known to the New South Africa as well as to the governments of the African countries which hosted the South African freedom fighters. It is evident that these children are going through an identity crisis in terms of their own understanding, particularly given that they were properly socialized by their South African fathers who made them feel South African. What is their current state of mind now that their fathers have not been heard of or from, since the 1980's, and not least, since the end of the repatriation period in 1994? And how would this current state of mind affect their right to live now as well as in the future as adults?. It is necessary to point out that African governments are morally bound to respond to the plight of these women and children.

The film also aims at disseminating critical information about recent positive- as well as not so positive- changes in governance to ordinary East Africans in a media format which is highly entertaining and moving. It is hoped that the proposed film project will inspire a large and diverse population of East Africans to strive for good governance in their own countries and to be able to better relate to developments elsewhere in Africa and in the rest of the world. In this regard, even though the primary audience for the proposed film are East Africans, it is hoped that the presentation of the subject matter in an entertaining and moving fashion would enable other African and international audiences to connect with the East African story as a human interest story. Ultimately, the idea is to reach and motivate large and diverse audiences through an entertainment format of a serious subject via established cinema halls, television broadcasting, mobile cinema vans, video libraries and clubs, as well as small showing in churches, NG0s and community based organizations.

13. Project Objectives

In undertaking this project, DTM's communication objectives are:

1. To popularize the debate on governance and human rights in East Africa through film.

2. To celebrate the contribution of East Africans to the process of democratization in East Africa in particular and Africa in general.
3. To acknowledge that good governance and democratic values are products of heroic sacrifices of ordinary individuals.
4. To motivate and challenge East Africans and increase their understanding of the critical role played by East Africa and other Africans, in the making of a new world in which democratic values are central to governance within and across Nations.
5. To talk in ordinary terms about the significance of East Africa in global affairs in general and with respect to South Africa in particular. This is important because a number of East Africans seem to be accepting media notions that East Africa lost its significance at the end of the cold war. Yet if the New South Africa continues to be a good story, then that story must also be good for a country like Tanzania because of the tremendous role played by the ordinary people in that country as well as those in other African countries towards the making of a New South Africa.
6. To accept that good governance is not only about state politics but that it is also if not primarily, about the sacrifices of ordinary people.
7. To promote mutual understanding and cooperation among East Africans and between them and other Africans, especially South Africans.
8. To develop and strengthen the capacity of independent and development oriented media in East Africa.

7.1 DEVELOPMENT THROUGH MEDIA: Progress Report

Dommie Yambo-Odotte

1. Introduction

FORGOTTEN, the feature film project that has been the centre of focus at DTM for more than a year now, is the first among a series of mass media projects that the organisation wishes to create out of research data. FORGOTTEN is a story about ordinary people in Africa and their often unrecognised and unappreciated contributions and sacrifices towards Africa's development. The research stage of the project that was conducted over a period of one year had stumbled upon the women and children in several

Africa countries who were associated with the struggle against apartheid but who now find themselves on the opposite side of the success story. It is around these women and children that a story about the ordinary people in Africa is being told. The story addresses many issues: issues of love and betrayal, betrayal by one's country; betrayal by a movement. It is a human rights story. It is a story that questions the violations of the rights to association. It raises pertinent questions regarding the real identities of the children resulting out of the association between exiled South African freedom fighters and the local women they associated with. In particular, since last October, the organisation has carried out various activities. These have included:

2. Further Research and Data Cross-Checking

Inspired by a desire to write all engaging, while at the same time objective story based on political and historical factual background, it was necessary that a process be designed that would allow for data cross checking as well as a rigorous screen play writing process. It is important to note here that this project addresses the issue regarding the devastation of antiapartheid activities elsewhere outside South Africa. It has been assumed that perhaps this is the first time that the struggle against apartheid will be looked at outside the generally assumed belief that the successful defeat of apartheid is the outcome of efforts from outside Africa. On the continent, it is only the efforts by South Africans themselves that have been lauded in reference to the spirited fight against apartheid. The role and the contributions of other Africans especially the contributions by ordinary people in Africa have often been ignored or misunderstood. Yet, it was precisely this role that was central not only to the struggle against apartheid as one of the most serious African problems in this century, but also as a struggle for democracy elsewhere on the continent as well. This contradicts the general belief that concern for democracy in East Africa is very recent, often traced back to the end of the cold war. It is indeed also true that ordinary people were already struggling for a better life and a better society long before then. Tanzania and other African countries started making sacrifices not only for their own country, but also for the liberation of South Africa long before the end of the cold war. This is the part of the story that is not often told. In fact, this is the side of the story that is much too often forgotten.

Through a human interest love story, FORGOTTEN the film will address issues on the ongoing political liberation and democratisation in East Africa, and its influence on the reconstruction and reconciliation process in South Africa, by raising the hitherto silent factors surrounding the effect of the anti apartheid struggle in countries where South African freedom fighters were exiled. The conclusions made from research data analysis reveal that there is a need to address the issue of the women and the children connected to former South African freedom fighters. What is now happening to them must be made known to the New South Africa to governments of African countries that hosted the South African freedom fighters, as well as to the international community. It is necessary to point out that the African governments and indeed the international community are morally bound to respond to the plight of these women and children.

3. From Research to Screen Play

Having made that research analysis, the screen play writing process commenced. This stage of the project has been particularly eager to produce a script with an entertainment value without loosing focus on the social message that the project aspires to deliver. To date, four official and almost ten unofficial drafts have been written. Each of the four official drafts have undergone critique sessions involving the creative team as well as other selected people including some members of the diplomatic corp. Mostly these people have appreciated what the project aims to achieve. They have been both surprised and particularly appreciative of the new information that the project presents. We are now convinced that we have put together an engaging and politically strong script. Most importantly, we believe that this is a critical story that must be brought to the screen. Although the current draft is nearly the final draft, we are however aware that further re-writing of the screen play will still be undertaken. As is usually the case in film projects, changes in screen plays call still be made even during location filming. Besides this film is being produced for mass consumption. It is paramount that views from elsewhere are taken into account particularly at script writing stage when the making of changes is likely to be less expensive. Sharing the script with different people has also been particularly undertaken at this stage in an attempt to establish audience response, and the overall appeal that the finished film will have on the target audience. So far, the reception has been good with some very encouraging media reviews as well. Going by the enquiries that have come through our office, it is our belief that the film will make a significant impact particularly as an African film project, as well as the filming transition of an all important and yet to be addressed issue into a mass media project for awareness creation.

4. From Screen Play to 35mm Feature Film

On the 9th of October [1998] we have scheduled a Screen Play Reading Session as part of an advisory panel meeting. The script will be read by a few selected performing artists after which the advisory panel will present their screen play analysis reports. The advisory panel, selected from five countries, are already in possession of the screen play and are in the process of preparing a critical and objective analysis for presentation during the meeting.

The pre-production office opens thereafter- about the 15th of October 1998. During this time, we will conclude crewing process. This is the stage in which we will conclude the selection of the rest of the production team members, the cast, location selection and all other aspects that fall within this stage. The end of this stage will lead into the production stage.

5. Future Direction: Vision and Sustainability

Beyond the release of the film, DTM has already embarked on a strategic distribution planning with the express aim of making sure that the film reaches the targeted audience through out Africa as well as the rest of the world.

Besides this particular film project, DTM believes that there is an urgent need to begin a process that can allow research data to be accessible to the ordinary people. It is DTM's belief that one of the greatest hindrance in the development movement is the lack of effective participation of the civil society. This is mainly because information on development aspirations are yet to be effectively disseminated to civil society in ways that they can easily understand and identify with. While this information may have effectively served their academic and policy purposes, they must also begin to permeate the civil society circles. One of the best ways to realise this is to access the same information through translating them into audio-visual products. The audio-visual media, as we all know, is a medium that can appeal to all sorts of audiences across the academic board. Such products can be distributed for mass consumption through broadcast establishments as well as through the mushrooming media outlets that are now beginning to reach many more audiences include those in the grassroots. At the same time, the same products can further be used to express as well as share the region's hopes and aspirations with the rest of the continent as well as the rest of the world.

6. Sustainability

In the process of disseminating its programs, DTM hopes to raise some finances from sales and distributor rights. This will in turn be re-invested into the production of other audio-visual products as indicated in DTM's production forecast. This include the much talked about and yet to be realised weekly radio and television current affairs programme titled: **EAST AFRICA TODAY**. DTM is also currently exploring other feature film project ideas. Unfortunately, the audio-visual media industry is an expensive one. Because of this, DTM will still require financial assistance for sometime before it is able to be self-sustaining. We have commenced the putting together of a five year business plan which, we hope, will present us with a clearer picture of future sustainability.

7. Synergy Strategies

Regarding synergy strategies within the New Africa Initiative, DTM appreciates that the Partners in Initiatives are currently engaged in very exciting projects. These projects must however be shared with others outside the Initiative itself. The organisation believes that many more people in East Africa, the rest of the continent as well as the international community must also begin to appreciate the initiative's ideals and aspirations. The audio-visual media is an effective way to realise this. Within the EAST AFRICA TODAY, the production of a weekly or monthly radio and television programs will complement others products like SAREAT's proposed newsletter among others. This would mean that DTM is in constant touch with all the NAI partners in order to establish the aspects in each initiative that may from time to time require such services. To realise this, DTM must place itself in a position that allows it a state of preparedness with equipment and ability to be on call at all times for the NAI partners. This can also include other development project that are currently taking place in the region, the continent and elsewhere. Through this arrangement, DTM also would like to pursue its other wish to create training opportunities for a new generation of film makers who will pursue further the wish to produce films with social messages in ways that will educate as they entertain audiences.

DISCUSSION AND EXCHANGE OF VIEWS (DTM)

The presentation of this paper has generated discussion on wide-ranging issues. Questions, comments and suggestions were entertained. Among the major problems identified was the low TV per capita in Africa. To overcome this problem with a view particularly to reaching rural people, it was suggested that contacts should be established with Outreach Africa. Access to TV was an essential prerequisite to the use of the film medium as a tool for the dissemination of ideas.

It was proposed that particular attention should be given to the feature film FORGOTTEN because it is a good instrument to show the hitherto forgotten aspects of the anti-apartheid struggle to the wider public. It highlights the contributions of the poor African countries to the success of the struggle. It directs attention to the heroic, yet unsung, contributions of ordinary African men and women to the movement. Moreover, even if apartheid has bowed out of the public stage, it is still necessary to prepare a comprehensive documentary on it for the purpose of posterity. Even if the presentation focused on Tanzania and to a certain extent on Zambia and Kenya, attention was drawn from the floor to Ethiopian contributions to the struggle which could by no means be dismissed as insignificant. Military training was given by Ethiopia to a number of African liberation movements which included that of South Africa. The training given to Mandela in that country was pointed out as the most illustrious case.

In the film, sustained attempts must be made to explore the unique approach of Tanzania to the refugee problem- while other countries put them in camps, the Tanzanians allowed them to mix freely with the civilian population. This had a big impact on the morale and well-being of the refugees while it also led to more enduring interactions with the local people. Marriage to which the feature film draws attention was one of the salient features of this interaction.

A large number of other questions were also raised. That the distribution of TV sets was limited had been noted. Rather than waiting until it reached the wider public, particularly the rural population, it was suggested that other media should be explored for reaching the population. Video was suggested as a good intermediary. But then the film should be shown not only to the wider public but also to policy makers who should be involved also. Questions were also raised on the proposed linkage between DTM and the partners of the New African Initiative in pursuing the objectives of N.A.I.

It was believed in conclusion that these vibrant discussions and the suggestions forwarded would enrich the proposal of the DTM further.

8

EVALUATION AND SYNERGY

1. Evaluating Our Work: Measuring Impact

The issue of evaluating performance and measuring impact relating to the different components of the NAI was raised during the workshop sessions. Several participants noted that this is an undertaking of paramount importance whose proper implementation could lead to the realization of stated goals and objectives.

It was expressed that both evaluation and impact assessment could be based on such things as internal and external indicators of success, strategies for sharing information, and the expectations of beneficiaries and stakeholders.

Realising flawless implementation of planned activities, creating efficient mechanisms for distributing resources and entrenching a good deal of integration within internal systems and structures were identified as internal indicators of success. The external indicators were listed as the level of community awareness about program components, the extent of requests and demands by beneficiaries/stakeholders for the expansion of services and activities, and the degree of appreciation on the part of donors of what has been undertaken.

Identifying/selecting key contact persons and instituting steering committees that represent the different program components within the NAI were viewed as useful strategies to facilitate the smooth flow of information. It was envisaged that both the contact persons and the steering committees can provide detailed information on developments within projects. In this regard, creating a web-site was considered as one option for sharing information effectively.

It was underlined that joint action could result in making activities cost-effective (economy of scale), facilitate information sharing, and entail wider exposure for those involved. It was noted that making regular interaction, and developing a habit of mutual respect creates the best environment for working together. On the other hand, such barriers as personal ego and rivalry, lack of interest, and poor infrastructure of communication can undermine the possibility of success for joint endeavors.

2. Creating Synergy: Strategies for Collaborative Action

The organisers of the workshops scheduled allotted the final sessions to a discussion of the theme of synergy in order to brainstorm on strategies that will bring about smooth collaboration between the partners of New African Initiative. This was done because much weight was given to the need for collaborative action in light of the extreme scarcity of resources within which the component projects are going to operate. In this chapter, we present a brief summary of the major issues raised and discussed on the concluding sessions of the two workshops.

3. Concluding Session of the First Workshop

Collaborative action has many advantages. It enables Initiative partners to share resources and to provide support to each other. This will bring about economies of scale in the utilisation of resources. Duplication can be avoided- a concern that was repeatedly pointed out in the course of the conference. Initiative partners will bring about great cost effectiveness, if they pulled together their resources. Finally, collaborative action will enable them to reach a wider target group.

But then it was expressed in no uncertain terms that there are tough barriers to collaborative action. No room should be left open to illusions. Ego, sexism, personality differences and personality clashes, lack of shared values and poor communication networks were singled out as possible barriers to collaborative endeavours. Differences of goals and objectives as well as differences in values and attitudes, absence of culture of teamwork as well as scarcity of resources were identified as possible sources of friction and conflict that hamper collaboration. In addition, attention was drawn to legal and administrative hurdles, to weak infrastructures and to language barriers not only as serious impediments to smooth collaborative projects but also as constraints that intensify problems created by factors outlined earlier.

The meeting went on to identify possible correctives to these barriers. Mutual respect and sensitivity to each other's problems would help overcome the frictions that could be created. Regular interaction was also recommended as well as information sharing.
It was decided that the next meeting would provide the forum for evaluation of the work of partners and to hear annual progress reports and to look for

alternate funding sources. The issue of governance- focusing on an analysis of current governance and on indicators of governance- was suggested as a possible theme for the next gathering. It was believed that the analysis of experiences in collaborative action would enable participants to arrive at better *modus operandi.*

4. Concluding Session of the Second Workshop

This session also focused on how to create synergy among the Initiative partners. This synergy should strategically promote dialogue and identify issues that move the NAI forward. The critical challenge of NAI partners was in the re-examination of the common objectives, and from that analysis begin to set a course forward into a future that realizes the agenda being formulated today in East Africa. The presenters, Dr. Moyo and Dr. Robinson, articulated these aspects for such synergy and the need for a new vision for Africa through the East African eyes. Their presentations were elaborate and well-thought-out. Extensive discussions followed.

The question of inclusion of Ethiopia dominated the discussions as colleagues from Ethiopia felt the need for inclusion. Ethiopian colleagues articulated at length the desirability of Ethiopia being an integral part of the Initiative activities.

On both workshops, issues were raised in the speeches of the presenters about the New African and about the need for the way forward. It was also suggested that the way forward could not be found unless a new definition of a new Africa was found. It seemed apparent that the project by National Museums of Kenya (NMK) offered some answers, but more was done into the past culture to find that definition of new Africa.

As the discussions continued participants pondered over the way forward, others posed the question of relevancy. Discussions revolved round the issue of how to locate the Initiative with the context of what was going on in East Africa, on the whole continent and globally. It was therefore felt that the Initiative ought to relate to what was going on in society. To achieve this, it was suggested that the Initiative had to find a direct link with struggles relating to democratic questions, questions about Africa's role in the international economic system, and unless that was done, the Initiative could remain an academic exercise.

Then exchanges of ideas ensued on each project. Observations, comments, suggestions were forwarded on each of them in a very detailed manner. The central theme of the discussions were synergy issues - focusing on strategies for collaborative action. The need to co-ordinate fund raising activities to avoid unnecessary competition among Initiative components from similar funding sources was identified as one of the major barriers to collaborative action. The Steering Committee of the NAI was advised to look seriously into the issue of fund-raising. It was advised to allocate funds to different components of the Initiative with the view to sustain all NAI programmes.

ANNEX I

The New Africa Initiative Workshop
"Working for Synergy"

October 12 - 14, 1997, Imperial Hotel, Addis Ababa, Ethiopia

List of Participants

PRESENTERS

---

(1) **Ms. Dommie Yambo-Odotte**
Development Through Media
PO Box 34696
Nairobi, Kenya

Tel: 00-254-2-228459; 331414; 240625 (o)
Fax: 00-254-2-228464
00-254-2-444488 (h)

(2) **Mr. Ngunyi Ngunyi**
Series on Alternative Research in East Africa (SARET)
PO Box 72289
Nairobi, Kenya

Tel: 00-254-2-717345 (o)
Fax: 00-254-2-719918
00-254-2-723593 (h)

(3) **Dr. John J. Barya**
Kituo Cha Katiba
PO Box 9863
Kampala, Uganda

Tel: 00-256-41-242987; 231228; 341358 (O)
Fax: 00-256-41-235413

(4) **Professor Rwekaza Mukandala**
Uongozi School
PO Box 35042
Dar es Salaam, Tanzania

Tel: 00-255-51-43130 (o)
Cel: 0812-780694
Fax: 00-255-51-43078/43395
00-255-51-43195 (h)

REPRESENTING PRINCIPAL ORGANIZATION GROUPS IN THE NEW AFRICA INITIATIVE

(5) **Professor Andrew S. Kiondo**
Uongozi School
Department of Political Science and Public Administration
University of Dar es Salaam
PO Box 35042
Dar es Salaam, Tanzania

Tel: 00-255-51-43130 (h)
00-255-51-48348 (h)
Fax: 00-255-41-43130/43395

(6) **Professor Edmond Keller**
Uongozi School
The James S. Coleman
African Studies Center
University of California, Los Angeles
10244 Bunche Hall
PO Box 951310
Los Angeles, CA 90095-1310
U.S.A.

Tel: 00-1-310- 825-3779 (o)
Fax: 00-1-310-206-2250

(7) **Professor Joshua Olewe Nyunya**
Uongozi School
IDIS
University of Nairobi
PO Box 30197
Nairobi, Kenya

Tel: 00-254-2-339014
Fax: 00-254-2-339014

(8) **Professor A.B. Mujaju**
Uongozi School
Department of Political Science
Makerere University
PO Box 7062
Kampala, Uganda

Tel: 00-256-41-531499
Fax: 00-256-41-531481

(9) **Professor Foster Byarugaba**
Uongozi School
Department of Political Science
Makerere University
PO Box 7062
Kampala, Uganda

Tel: 00-256-41-531499
Fax: 00-256-41-531481

(10) **Dr. Rose Migiro**
Kituo Cha Katiba
Women's Legal Aid Center
PO Box 10463
Dar es Salaam, Tanzania

Tel: 00-255-51-43254
Cel: 0812 782203,
Fax: 00-255-51-668147

REPRESENTING REFERENCE GROUP IN THE NEW AFRICA INITIATIVE

(11) **Ms. Helen Kijo-Bisimba**
Legal and Human Rights Centre
PO Box 45076
Dar es Salaam, Tanzania

Tel/Fax: 00-255-51-113177

(12) **Ms. Tumaini Silaa**
Tanzania Women Lawyers Association
PO Box 9460
Dar es Salaam, Tanzania

Tel: 00-255-51-113626; 23119 (o)

(13) **Ms. Assumpta Oturu**
Radio Station KPFK
(Development Through Media)
12400 Ventura Blvd, Suite 353
Studio City, CA. 91604
U.S.A.

Tel: 00-1-818-985 2711 (o)
Fax: 00-1-818-980 0901

(14) **Mr. Bernard Luanda**
Senior Deputy Registrar
Court of Appeal of Tanzania
PO Box 9004
Dar es Salaam,Tanzania

Tel: 00-255- 51-116654 (o)

(15) **Dr. Joy Kwesiga**
Action for Development
PO Box 16729
Kampala, Uganda

Tel: 00-256-41-532311; 531484
Fax: 00-256-41-530460

(16) **Mr. A. K. D. Odoch**
Office of the Prime Minister
Republic of Uganda
PO Box 341
Kampala, Uganda

Tel: 00-256-41-232575; 258741 (o)
Fax: 00-256-41-241139

(17) **Ms. Atsango Chesoni**
International Federation of Women Lawyers
PO Box 46324
Nairobi, Kenya

Tel: 00-254-2-717169 (o)
Fax: 00-254-2-716840

(18) **Ms. Mildred Mkandla**
EarthCare Africa
PO Box 76358
Nairobi, Kenya

Tel: 00-254-2-564971 (o)
Fax: 00-254-2-562115

(19) **Mr. Ernest Zulu**
The United Republic of Tanzania
Tanzania Parliament
PO Box 9133

Dar es Salaam, Tanzania

Tel: 00-255-51-118591 (o)
Fax: 00-255-51-112538

(20) **Ato Kassahun Berhanu**
Political Science and International Relations Department
Addis Ababa University
PO Box 1176
Addis Ababa, Ethiopia

Tel: 00-251-1-117849 (o)

(21) **Ato Paulos Chane**
Management & Public Administration Department
Addis Ababa, University
PO Box 1176
Addis Ababa, Ethiopia

Tel: 00-251-1-117278 (o)

(22) **Ato Zekarias Keneaa**
Law School
Addis Ababa University
PO Box 1176
Addis Ababa, Ethiopia

Tel: 00-251-1-111733 (o)

(23) **Ethiopian Women Lawyers Association**
PO Box 13760
Addis Ababa, Ethiopia

Tel: 00-251-1-158666 (o)

SESSION CHAIRS

(24) **Professor Jassy B. Kwesiga**
Development Network of Indigenous Voluntary Associations
PO Box 11224
Kampala, Uganda

Tel: 00-256-41-530575 (o)
Fax: 00-256-41-531236
(Development Through Media)

(25) **Professor Kadmiel Wekwete**
United Centre for Human Settlements
PO Box 30030
Nairobi, Kenya

Tel: 00-254-2-623771 (o)
Fax: 00-254-2-624266/7
(National Museums of Kenya)

(26) **Professor J.K. Kimura**
Institute of Policy Analysis and Research
PO Box 45843
Nairobi, Kenya

Tel: 00-254-2-251179; 251162 (o)
Fax: 00-254-2-251162
(Series on Alternative Research in East Africa Trust)

(27) **Visiting Professor Pearl Robinson**
Makerere University
Department of Political Science and Public Administration
PO Box 7062
Kampala, Uganda

Tel: 00-256-41-531499 (o)
Fax: 00-256-41- 534181

Director International Relations Programs and
Associate Professor or Political Science
Tufts University
International Relations Program
605 Cabot Hall
Medford, MA 02155
U.S.A.

Tel: 00-617-628-5000
Fax: 00-617-627-3083
(Uongozi School)

(28) **Ms. MaryKay Penn**
Venzen Ross Consulting
44 Hamilton Terrace
New York, NY 10031
U.S.A.

Tel: 00-1-212-234 4197 (o)
Fax: 00-1-212-234 7978
(Kituo Cha Katiba)

RAPPORTEURS

(29) **Mr. Nathan Byamukama**
Uganda Human Rights Commission
PO Box 4929
Kampala, Uganda

Tel: 00-256-41-348006/8 (o)
Fax: 00-256-41-255261

(30) **Mr. Sabiti Makara**
Makerere University
Department of Political Science
PO Box 7062
Kampala, Uganda

Tel: 00-256-41-531499 (o)
Fax: 00-256-41-534181

(31) **Ms. Muriel Mafico**
The Institute of Development Studies
PO Box 880
Causeway, Harare
Zimbabwe

Tel: 00-263-4-307900/6 (o)
Fax: 00-263-4-333345

(32) **Mr. Anthony Masendeke**
University of Zimbabwe
146 Westwood Park
PO Box Kambuzuma
Harare, Zimbabwe
Tel: 00-263-4-229673 (h)

(33) **Mr. Geoffrey Tukahebwa**
Department of Political Science
Makerere University
PO Box 7062
Kampala, Uganda

Tel: 00-256-41-531499 (o)
Fax: 00-256-41-534181

(34) **Ms. Catherine Njau**
AISEC Kenya
PO Box 30197
Nairobi, Kenya

Tel/Fax: 00-254-2-245135 (o)

(35) **Ms. Cheryl Cooper**
International Federation of Women Lawyers (FIDA)
PO Box 46324
Nairobi, Kenya

Tel: 00-254-2-717169; 711853; 714629 (o)
Fax: 00-254-2-716840

CONVENOR

(36) Organization for Social Science Research (OSSREA)
PO Box 31971
Addis Ababa, Ethiopia

Tel: 00-251-1-119705
Fax: 00-251-1-551399

Contact Person: **Dr. Tegegne Teka**

FACILITATOR

(37) **Ms. MaryKay Penn**
Venzen Ross Consulting
44 Hamilton Terrace
New York, NY 10031
U.S.A.

Tel: 00-1-212-234 4197 (o)
Fax: 00-1-212-234 7978

FORD FOUNDATION

(38) **Dr. Nick Menzies**
The Ford Foundation
PO Box 41081
Nairobi, Kenya

Tel: 00-254-2-251814; 222298 (o)
Fax: 00-254-2-252830

(39) **Professor Jonathan N. Moyo**
The Ford Foundation
PO Box 41081
Nairobi, Kenya

Tel: 00-254-2-251814; 222298 (o)
Fax: 00-254-2-252830

SECRETARIAT

(40) **Ms. Zainab Ali**
The Ford Foundation
PO Box 41081
Nairobi, Kenya

Tel: 00-254-2-251814; 222298
Fax: 00-254-2-252830

(41) **Ms. Misrak Kinfemichael**
Organization for Social Science Research
in Eastern and Southern Africa
PO Box 31971
Addis Ababa, Ethiopia

Tel: 00-251-1-119705
Fax: 00-251-1-551399

ANNEX II

The New Africa Initiative (NAI) Workshop

4-7 October 1998, Safari Park Hotel, Nairobi, Kenya

List of Participants

ETHIOPIA

(1) **Ato Kassahun Berhanu**
Political Science and International Relations Department
Addis Ababa University
P. O. Box 1176
Addis Ababa, Ethiopia

Tel. 00-251-1-117849
C/o Fax: 00-251-1-551399

(2) **Ato Merera Gudina**
Political Science and International Relations Department
Addis Ababa University
P. O. Box 1176
Addis Ababa, Ethiopia

Tel. 00-251-1-117849
C/o Fax: 00-251-1-551399

(3) **Ato Paulos Chane**
Management and Public
Administration Department
Addis Ababa University
P. O. Box 1176
Addis Ababa, Ethiopia

Tel. 00-251-1-117278
C/o Fax: 00-251-1-551399

KENYA

(4) **Ms. Dommie Yambo-Odotte**
Producer, Development Through Media
P. O Box 34696
Nairobi, Kenya

Tel. 00-254-2-228459/331414
Fax: 00-254-2-228464

(5) **Ms. Mildred Mkandla**
EarthCare Africa
P. O. Box 76358
Nairobi, Kenya

Tel. 00-254-2-564971
Fax: 00-254-2-562115

(6) **Professor Joshua Olewe Nyunya**
Uongozi School
IDIS
University of Nairobi
P. O. Box 30197
Nairobi, Kenya

Tel. 00-254-2-339014
Fax: 00-254-2-336885

(7) **Mr. Mutahi Ngunyi**
The Series on Alternative Research in East Africa
P. O. Box 6038
Nairobi, Kenya

Tel. 00-254-2-217382
Fax: 00-254-2-719918/723593

(8) **Mr. Dauti Kahura**
SAREAT
P. O. Box 6038
Nairobi, Kenya

(9) **Mr. Karuti Kanyinga**
IDS
University of Nairobi
P. O. Box 30197
Nairobi, Kenya

Tel.: 00-254-2-581805
00-254-2-337436
Fax: 00-254-2-222036

(10) **Dr. Mohamed Isahakia**
Director General
National Museums of Kenya
P. O. Box 40658
Nairobi, Kenya

Tel. 00-254-2-448929/448931
742131/742161
Fax: 00-254-2-741424/566739

(11) **Dr. Sultan Somjee**
National Museums of Kenya
P. O. Box 40658
Nairobi, Kenya

Tel. 00-254-2-742131/742161
Fax: 00-254-2-741424

(12) **Ms. Connie Gondi-Hughton**
C/o SAREAT
P. O. Box 6038
Nairobi, Kenya

(13) **Prof. Njuguna Ngethe**
Institute of Policy Analysis and Research
P. O. Box 45843
Nairobi, Kenya

Tel: 00-254-2-334244
E-mail: ids@nbnet.co.ke

(14) **Prof. John O. Shiundu**
Vice President, OSSREA and
Registrar (Administration)
Kenyatta University
P. O. Box 43844
Nairobi, Kenya

Tel. 00-254-2-811196
Fax: 00-254-2-811575

(15) **Mr. John Aluko Orodho**
Liaison Officer for OSSREA
Kenyatta University
P. O. Box 43844
Nairobi, Kenya

Tel. 00-254-2-81162Ext. 57499
Fax: 00-254-2-811575

SOUTH AFRICA

(16) **Prof. Jonathan N. Moyo**
University of Witwatersrand
Private Bag 3
Wits 2050
Johanneburg, South Africa

Tel. 00-27-11-7820407/3262997
Fax No. 00-27-11-7820133

TANZANIA

(17) **Professor Rwekaza Mukandala**
Chairman, Uongozi School and Dean
P. O. Box 35042
Dar es Salaam, Tanzania

Tel. 00-255-51-410510/410501 Ext. 2294
Fax: 00-255-51-410395

(18) **Professor Andrew S. Kiondo**
Uongozi School
Department of Political Science and Public Administration
University of Dar es Salaam
P. O. Box 35042
Dar es Salaam, Tanzania

Tel. 00-255-51-410130/
410348/0811334941
Fax: 00-255-5-410357

(19) **Ms. Helen Kijo-Bisimba**
Legal and Human Rights Centre
P. O. Box 75254
Dar es Salaam, Tanzania

Tel. 00-255-51-113177
Fax: 00-255-51-113177

(20) **Ms. Vupe Ligate**
Tanzania Women Lawyers Association
P. O. Box 9460
Dar es Salaam, Tanzania

Tel. 00-255-51-110758
Fax: 00-255-51-118974

(21) **Mr. Ernest Zulu**
United Republic of Tanzania
Parliament of Tanzania
P. O. Box 9133
Dar es Salaam, Tanzania

Tel.00-255-51-112065/812785839
Fax: 00-255-51-112538

(22) **Dr. Deo Rugaimukamu**
Project Administrator
EAFU
P. O. Box 35039
Dar es Salaam, Tanzania

(23) **Ms. Stella Njuu**
Coopted Member
EUFUI Organizing Committee
P. O. Box 35039
Dar es Salaam, Tanzania

(24) **Ms. Bernadetta Killian**
EAFUI
P. O. Box 35039
Dar es Salaam, Tanzania

Tel.: 00-255-0812-789606

UGANDA

---

(25) **Ms. Harriet Busingye**
Acting Director
KITUO CHA KATIBA
P. O. Box 3277
Kampala, Uganda

Tel. 00-256-41-251717
Fax: 00-256-41-251717

(26) **Dr. John J. Barya**
Director, CBR
Kituo Cha Katiba
P. O. Box 9863
Kampala, Uganda

Tel. 00-256-41-342897/231228
Fax: 00-256-41-235413

(27) **Professor A. B. Mujaju**
Uongozi School
Department of Political Science
Makerere University
P. O. Box 7062
Kampala, Uganda

Tel. 00-256-41-531499
Fax: 00-256-41-534181

(28) **Professor Foster Byarugaba**
Uongozi School
Department of Political Science
Makerere University
P. O. Box 7062
Kampala, Uganda

Tel. 00-256-41-531499
Fax: 00-256-41-534181

(29) **Ms. Juliet Bintu**
Coopted Member
Faculty of Social Sciences
Makerere University
P. O. Box 7062
Kampala, Uganda

(30) **Mr. Geoffrey Tukahebwa**
Department of Political Science
Makerere University
P. O. Box 7062
Kampala, Uganda

Tel. 00-256-41-531499
Fax: 00-256-41-534181

(31) **Prof. Ruth Mukama**
Chair, ACFODE
P. O. Box 16729
Kampala, Uganda

(32) **Mr. A. K. D. Odoch**
Office of the Prime Minister
Republic of Uganda
P. O. Box 341
Kampala, Uganda

Tel. 00-256-41-232575/258741
Fax: 00-256-41-241139

(33) **Mr. Nathan Byamukama**
Uganda Human Rights Commission
P. O. Box 4929
Kampala, Uganda

Tel. 00-256-41-348006/8
Fax: 00-256-41-255261

(34) **Mr. Sabiti Makara**
Makerere University
Department of Political Science
P. O. Box 7062
Kampala, Uganda

Tel. 00-256-41-531499
Fax: 00-256-41-534181

USA

(35) **Professor Edmond Keller**
Uongozi School
The James S. Coleman
African Studies Center
University of California, Los Angeles
10244 Bunche Hall
P. O. Box 951310
Los Angeles, CA 90095-1310, USA

Tel. 00-1-310-565 1234
Fax: 00-1-310-206 2250

(36) **Ms. Assumpta Oturu**
Radio Station KPFK
(Development Through Media)
12400 Ventura Blvd, Suite 353
Studio City, CA. 91604
USA

Tel. (818) 508-9254 (Res)
(818) 508-4377 (Off.)
E-mail:oturu@earthlink.net

(37) **Prof. Pearl T. Robinson**
Department of Political Science
Tufts University
Medford, Massachusetts
USA

Tel. 00-1-617-628-5000 Ext. 72776
Fax No. 00-1-617-627-3660

ZIMBABWE

(38) **Mr. Anthony F. Masendeke**
University of Zimbabwe
146 Westwood Park
P. O. Box Kambuzuma
Harare, Zimbabwe

Tel. 00-263-4-790801/7
Fax: 00-263-4-795220

FORD FOUNDATION

(39) **Dr. Katherine Pearson**
Representative
The Ford Foundation
P. O. Box 41081
Nairobi, Kenya

Tel. 00-254-2-222298
Fax: 00-254-2-252830

(40) **Dr. Tade Akin Aina**
Program Officer
Governance and Civil Society Program
The Ford Foundation
P. O. Box 41081
Nairobi, Kenya

Tel. 00-254-2-222298
Fax: 00-254-2-252830

IDRC

(41) **Dr. Eva Rathegeber**
Regional Director
IDRC
P. O. Box 62084
Nairobi, Kenya

OSSREA

(42) **Dr. Tegegne Teka**
Regional Project Coordinator
OSSREA
P. O. Box 31971
Addis Ababa, Ethiopia

Fax No. 00-251-1-551399
Tel. No. 00-251-1-551163/553281
E-mail: ossrea@telecom.net.et

(43) **Prof. Abdel Ghaffar M. Ahmed**
Executive Secretary
OSSREA
P. O. Box 31971
Addis Ababa, Ethiopia

Fax No. 00-251-1-551399
Tel. No. 00-251-1-551163/553281
E-mail: ossrea@telecom.net.et

(44) **Ms. Misrak Kinfemichael**
Senior Secretary
OSSREA
P. O. Box 31971
Addis Ababa, Ethiopia
Fax No. 00-251-1-551399
Tel. No. 00-251-1-551163/553281
E-mail: ossrea@telecom.net.et

(45) **Ms. Birkababa Wolde**
Accountant
OSSREA
P. O. Box 31971
Addis Ababa,Ethiopia

Fax No. 00-251-1-551399
Tel. No. 00-251-1-551163/553281
E-mail: ossrea@telecom.net.et

INVITED

(46) **Dr. John Mugabe**
Executive Director
African Centre for Technology Studies
P. O. Box 45917
Nairobi, Kenya

Tel. 00-254-2-577152/577175
Fax: 00-254-2-573002

(47) **Dr. Willy Mutunga**
C/o SAREAT
P. O. Box 72289
Nairobi, Kenya

(48) **Dr. Janet Macharia**
UNIFEM, NBO
C/o Development Through Media
P. O. Box 34696
Nairobi, Kenya

(49) **Professor Kadmiel Wekwete**
United Centre for Human Settlements
P. O. Box 30030
Nairobi, Kenya

Tel. 00-254-2-623771
Fax: 00-254-2-624266/7

(50) **Professor J. K. Kimura**
Institute of Policy Analysis and Research
P. O. Box 45843
Nairobi, Kenya
Tel. 00-254-2-251179/251162
Fax: 00-254-2-251162

(51) **Professor Kadmiel Wekwete**
United Centre for Human Settlements
P. O. Box 30030
Nairobi, Kenya
Tel. 00-254-2-623771
Fax: 00-254-2-624266/7

(52) **Professor J. K. Kimura**
Institute of Policy Analysis and Research
P. O. Box 45843
Nairobi, Kenya

Tel. 00-254-2-251179/251162
Fax: 00-254-2-251162

(53) **Ms. Jean Kamau**
Executive Director
International Federation of Women Lawyers
P. O. Box 46324
Nairobi, Kenya

Tel. 00-254-2-717169, 711853
Fax: 00-254-2-716840

(54) **Sida Representative**
Swedish Embassy
P. O. Box 220863
Nairobi, Kenya

(55) **The Representative**
DANIDA
Rehani House (HFCK)
Kenyatta Avenue
P. O. Box 40412
Nairobi, Kenya

(56) **The Representative**
The Rockfeller Foundation
P. O. Box 47543
Nairobi, Kenya

(57) **Mr. Daniel Davis**
Institution Development Officer
British Development Division in Eastern Africa
Upper Hill Road
P. O. Box 30465
Nairobi, Kenya

(58) **Hon. Justice L. Kalegeya**
Tanzania High Court
P. O. Box 9004
Dar es Salaam, Tanzania

(59) **Ms. Willie Pronk**
Senior Policy Officer
Human Rights
Rammweg 16
2596 HL Den Haag
The Netherlands

(60) **Hon. Lady Justice Solomy B. Bossa (Mrs.)**
KITUO CHA KATIBA
P. O. Box 3277
Kampala, Uganda

(61) **Prof. Stephen Ndegwa**
The College of William and Mary
Morton Hall
Department of Government
Williamsburg, VA 23187-8795
USA

Printed in the United Kingdom
by Lightning Source UK Ltd.
122322UK00001B/85-94/A